ANN CARTWRIGHT

Forty Short Plays

Plays and Sketches for the Classroom

Heinemann Educational Publishers
Halley Court, Jordan Hill, Oxford OX2 8EJ
Part of Harcourt Education

8

10-digit ISBN: 0-435233-27-0
13-digit ISBN: 978-0-435233-27-3

Original design by Jeffrey White Creative Associates; adapted by Jim Turner
Typeset by 🅐 Tek-Art, Croydon, Surrey
Cover photography by Tony Stone Images
Cover design by Philip Parkhouse Design Consultancy
Printed and bound in the United Kingdom by Clays Ltd, St Ives plc

For *Josephine, Eric, Jan, Chris, David, Jonathan and Ken with love*

CONTENTS

(Note: the number of characters in each piece is given in parentheses.)

Scripts

1 Audition (3)	3
2 Fish (2)	6
3 When (1)	9
4 Crush (1)	11
5 Forgetting (4)	13
6 Bullies (4)	17
7 Fault (2)	21
8 Pumpkin (1)	24
9 Pocket-money (6)	28
10 Order (6)	34
11 Fans (4)	40
12 Away (6)	45
13 Us (6)	58
14 Friends (6)	64
15 Caring (4)	72
16 Frustration (4)	78
17 Gents (3)	85
18 Gender (6)	90
19 Grounded (4)	97
20 Common (2)	103

Sketches

1	Thinking (2)	113
2	Place (3)	114
3	Stuck (2)	116
4	Programme (4)	118
5	Itch (2)	120
6	Chit-chat (2)	122
7	Class (3)	124
8	Ownership (2)	126
9	Fate (3)	128
10	There (2)	130
11	Move (3)	132
12	Clever (4)	134
13	Fashion (2)	136
14	Love (2)	137
15	Fancy (2)	138
16	Too (3)	139
17	Queue (4)	140
18	File (2)	141
19	Quiet (2)	142
20	Peace (2)	143

Activities   147

INTRODUCTION

This collection of scripts is designed to assist the classroom teacher in widening the reading of Key Stage 3 pupils in English and drama. The book comprises a variety of sketches for solo, paired and grouped work. The range of issues will:

- stimulate pupils' awareness and approach to issues raised in the scripts
- provide stimulus for interpretation of character and meaning
- supply material for use in Literacy sessions.

There is also a collection of workshop sketches which pupils, through discussion, must interpret themselves as no indication of character or setting is given.

The activities accompanying the scripts are to further pupils' own discussion, reading and writing skills.

I hope this collection proves to be a useful resource to the busy classroom teacher.

Ann Cartwright

Scripts

AUDITION

Cast: *Director*, a woman
Actor 1, female
Actor 2, male

Scene: *A theatre director auditioning acts.*

Director (*bored, seen too many acts already*) How many are left, Baz? Two? Thank God. My garbage threshold is on overload. Next!

Actor 1 (*rushes forward, dead keen*) Hello! I'd like to read from –

Director (*emphatically*) Name?

Actor 1 Erm – erm – can't remember – wait a second –

Director Good grief.

Actor 1 No – yes, I can! Got it! Marie Connor! Phew!

Director Previous experience?

Actor 1 Experience? Erm – well – I had a pretty nasty experience on the bus the other day when my handbag burst open and I had to crawl around under the seats –

Director Acting experience, Ms Connor.

Actor 1 Oh! Well, I've been in Bognor Rep for three seasons, (*lying somewhat*) done a few commercials, (*getting more daring, watching Director writing everything down*) got squatters' rights on *EastEnders*, got shot on *Brookside*, (*total dare*) and worked with Tom Cruise.

Director (*stops writing in disbelief*) Tom Cruise?

Actor 1 Did I say Tom Cruise? I meant Tom Jones. In Las Vegas. I was one of his dancers.

Director You dance?

Actor 1 Oh, yes. Like a dream.

Director (*calling her bluff*) Go ahead.

Actor 1	What? Now?
Director	Yes.
Actor 1	But – I was going to read. From *Hamlet*.
Director	Do both.
Actor 1	At the same time?
Director	Why not? That isn't a problem, is it, Ms Connor, being as versatile as you undoubtedly are?
Actor 1	(*panicking*) No. No – problem. Erm – 'To be, or not to be' (*leaps about a bit like on a work-out video*) 'That is the question.' (*claps and goes down on one knee*)
Director	Next!
Actor 1	Was that no good?
Director	No good? Ms Connor – if you've danced at Las Vegas with Tom Jones, I've done The Full Monty in Safeway!
Actor 1	Have you? Did you get good reviews?
Director	Next!!
	Actor 1 exits. Actor 2 enters in an anorak and woolly hat. He has poor sight and poor hearing.
Actor 2	Is this the stage?
Director	Good grief. Another one. – (*tiredly patient*) Ye – es.
Actor 2	Pardon?
Director	(*louder*) Yes. This is the stage.
Actor 2	Only I've come for the work, like.
Director	Name?
Actor 2	Eh?
Director	NAME?!
Actor 2	Oh. Brando.
Director	(*amazed to hear that name*) Brando?
Actor 2	That's right. Marvin Brando.
Director	After the famous actor?
Actor 2	No. After me Auntie Ursula.
Director	You got your stage-name from your Auntie Ursula?

So it was Ursula Brando?

Actor 2 No. Bickerstaff.

Director (*confused*) Bickerstaff?

Actor 2 A cracking woman was my Auntie Ursula. She was in show-business.

Director Really?

Actor 2 Played the spoons at the local social club. She did a lovely 'Y Viva España'. Did her knee in when she tried going classical. 'Flight of the Bumble Bee'. Nasty.

Director Moving on, Mr Brando – what theatrical experience have you had?

Actor 2 Theatrical what? What's that when it's at home?

Director Theatrical experience! Work in plays, television, theatre –

Actor 2 Oh. I play darts when the other lads let me. When they're nowhere near the board, like, seeing as I miss a lot. And I fixed a telly once. Only it blew up.

Director (*pause*) Mr Brando – why are you here?

Actor 2 To fix the stage. Loose board or something the chap on the 'phone said.

Director I thought you were auditioning!

Actor 2 What? I never touch the stuff.

Director Oh, I've had enough! Baz! Call Ms Connor back! She'll do! I'm off home for a gee-and-tee and a lie down!

She storms off.

Actor 1 (*enters*) Has she gone?

Actor 2 (*different accent – more 'refined'*) Off her head!

Actor 1 I got the job! Thanks, Uncle!

Actor 2 That's the last time I'm doing that dopey act to make you look good. (*taking off the anorak and hat*) Now, you put the anorak on. I fancy that Head Waiter's job at the Ritz.

They exit, Actor 1 hurriedly putting on the anorak and hat.

5

FISH

Cast: *Joey*
Goldie

Scene: *Two fish in an aquarium with a miniature castle in it. Joey, to begin with, is on his own.*

Joey   Just look at the time. Not a flake of fish-food in sight. (*looking out*) Oy! Kid! Pack in playing on your computer and feed me, will ya? – Hello. The other kid's just walked in. I'll get her attention. Wait a sec. She's carrying something. She's emptying it into the tank. Argh!

Goldie plunges in.

Goldie   Look out!

Joey   What's your game?

Goldie   Wow! Big tank! All right, are you?

Joey   Who the hell are you?

Goldie   I'm your new tank-mate!

Joey   I'm sorry. I live alone.

Goldie   Not any more, you don't. Wow! Look at that! They've got a castle!

He goes over to inspect it.

Joey   Oy! That's my place! You're trespassing!

Goldie   You're a bit uptight, aren't ya? Chill out, man, or your scales'll drop off.

Joey   This is totally out of order!

Goldie   Where do you kip, then? I'll take the turrets, if that's okay with you. I like the view.

Joey   You like the view? You're a fish, not a tourist! What are you doing here anyway?

Goldie   The little kid – the girl – she won me at the fair. Three ping-pong balls into three bowls and I was all hers. (*looking out*) Urgh! He's ugly. Who's that?

Joey	That's her brother. Watch out for him. When he gets bored he gets out the drinking straws and starts bubble-warfare.
Goldie	No!
Joey	When he's in a really bad mood, he has been known to suck up a third of the tank.
Goldie	What a monster!
Joey	The day he got a bad report from school, I nearly drowned in the shallows, I can tell you. And she's as bad. Emptied her pencil-case into the tank yesterday. Tried to colour me blue! Said that way I'd look like a tiny dolphin!
Goldie	How you must have suffered!
Joey	You'll never know.
Goldie	Look, I don't want to be any bother to you. If I'm really a problem, I'll just stay up the far end of the tank behind that coral. You won't even know I'm there. I'm very quiet. Just a few bubbles.
Joey	No. You're all right. We're in this thing together. I was getting a bit bored with my own company anyway, to tell you the truth. I can't even get fed on time. (*looking out*) Oy! Kid! Food! Food!!
Goldie	Ah, look. The little girl's coming over to feed us.
Joey	(*hides*) What? Agh!
Goldie	It's okay. No pencil-case. Just food.
Joey	Thank cod for that. – That's it, Girlie. Tip it in, whatever it is. Funny she's being kind for once. It's the dad that usually feeds me.
	Something plunges to the bottom of the tank like a bomb. The fish leap away from it.
Goldie	Agh! It's a bomb! It's a bomb! I'm too young to fry!
Joey	I knew it! Rotten kid! (*to Goldie*) Stay back! I'll check it out. (*takes a look*) It's all right. It's not a bomb.
Goldie	What is it, then?

Joey	It's a quarter of pineapple chunks. – Oy! Girlie! How are we supposed to eat these? They're like granite to us!
Goldie	Urgh! They'll melt and make the water go all cloudy. Then we'll get sugar-poisoning! Agh! Help!
Joey	Oh, shut up panicking, you! Here's the mother. – That's it, Love. Scoop 'em up.

Both fish leap back as the imaginary giant hand enters the tank to remove the sweets.

Goldie	Oo! Dish-wash hands!
Joey	It's her old man's turn to do the vacuuming this month.
Goldie	They take it in turns, do they?
Joey	I'll be glad when he's back on the dishes. He doesn't half give the bottom of our table a wallop with the Hoover every time he passes.
Goldie	I don't think I'm going to like it here.
Joey	You'll get used to it.
Goldie	I wish I was back at the fairground.
Joey	What? Stuffed in a plastic bag and hanging on a hook? Or maybe you'd like to be dead in a deep-freeze waiting to be eaten with some greasy chips?
Goldie	(*sulking*) I'm a goldfish, not a plaice.
Joey	Then count your blessings. (*looks up*) Eh, up. We're being fed at last! Manna from heaven! (*looking at Goldie, trying to be nice*) Go on. After you.
Goldie	Really?
Joey	Yeah. Eat up. Then after I'll give you a race round the castle.
Goldie	Cheers.

Goldie goes up to feed.

Joey	What did you say your name was?
Goldie	I didn't. It's Goldie.
Joey	I'm Joey. (*pause*) And don't eat all the big flakes. Tut! New fish on the block.

WHEN

Cast: *Jimmy, a young boy*

Scene: *Jimmy is sitting in his bedroom, surrounded by toys, books, posters, etc.*

Jimmy   (*to the audience*) You can come in if you like. – Sit there. – No! Not on my Manchester United cushion! You'll ruin it. – Yeah. There's all right. – When I get rich, I'm gonna get the duvet cover to match. And I'm gonna buy the club! It'll be great owning a football club. I'll get to go to all the games for free, meet all the players, go round with them after to . . . to . . . Oh, wherever it is they go. Not nightclubs, obviously, 'cause I'm too young at the moment, but when I get older, it'll be great. We'll all be mates, and they'll say 'Are you coming out with us, Jimmy?', and I'll say 'Yeah, I'll just get me coat.' It'll be great.

Jimmy hugs the cushion thoughtfully – then puts it to one side and picks up a catalogue. Starts leafing through it.

Jimmy   Look. When I get rich, I'm going to buy a load of stuff out of this catalogue. I'll buy this widescreen telly for me dad 'cause he loves the telly – when he's here. He works really hard, you see, so when he gets in from work he likes to go down the pub. Mum goes with him so my sister stops in with me. I'm in bed by the time they get back. But that's okay. They only work so hard because they love me. And when I'm rich, they'll be able to stay at home with me.

He closes the catalogue.

Jimmy   I'm not getting anything for my sister though. She's always telling me what to do. Do this, do that, eat your tea, I've spent ages cooking it. Then it starts again at bedtime! Put your pyjamas on, wash your face, brush your teeth, I could be out with my friends instead of looking after you, you know . . . Oh, it never ends! Girls!

He thinks, then opens the catalogue again.

Jimmy   Maybe just something small.

He goes to his piggy bank and shakes it.

Jimmy   I've got nearly five pounds saved up in here. I'm going to get me sister to buy a couple of lottery tickets with it for me – but she's got to bring me back the change. One for Wednesday and one for Saturday. I'm bound to win one of them 'cause Mum and Dad are always telling me I'm lucky. Lucky I've got them to look after me. Lucky to have a nice home. Lots of children are starving and living on the streets. Some kids have got to live at their nan's for being naughty. But not me. I'm lucky. And when I'm rich, it'll all be different.

He looks at the piggy bank.

Jimmy   Won't it?

He looks upset. Suddenly throws his piggy bank across the room and smashes it.

CRUSH

Cast: *Margie, a little girl*

Scene: *The corner of a primary school playground.*
Margie takes the audience into her confidence.

Margie   Can you see him? He's over there. There. Next to
Jacqueline. – Jacqueline Mason. My best friend. –
No! Don't stare at him! He'll see you're looking.

She gets sweets out of her pocket.

Margie   Do you want a sweet? He gave them to me
yesterday, but I'll let you have one. Just one. – No!
One! – Put that one back. I saw you. – I'm going to
keep at least one of them for ever. As a keepsake.

She puts the sweets back in her pocket.

Margie   I love Marcus Jordaine. He's so lovely. He has very
straight teeth – except for that gap at the front. But
his second teeth will be coming in very soon, so he
won't look like a letter-box any more. And he's got
ever such pretty hair – all curly like a mop.

She gets out a Valentine's card and shows it to the
audience.

Margie   I also love him because he's kind. Look. He gave
me this. We had to make them in class yesterday
and I was having trouble sticking the hearts on, so
he helped me. When we'd finished them, the
teacher said we could either take them home or
give them to someone in the class that we liked.
Horrible Ian Turton gave his to Samantha Fellows,
saying she ought to keep it as it was prettier than
she was. But she got him back at playtime. She
rubbed about six Jammie Dodgers into his hair. The
teacher went mad at both of them.

She looks lovingly at the card.

Margie   But Marcus just walked up to me with his card – in
front of the whole class – and said I was very nice

and he wanted me to have his card. The class all giggled – but I didn't care. – I'm putting it away now in case it rains. I don't want it getting smudged.

She puts card away.

Margie   He looked after me the other day as well. I fell over in the playground and hurt my hand. Look. Right there. See? He helped me up and took me to the teacher. It was really sore, but I didn't cry or anything. The teacher cleaned my hand for me, but she let Marcus put the plaster on.

She looks at her hand.

Margie   It didn't hurt at all after that.

She looks back to the audience.

Margie   My mum says I'm being silly and it's just a crush. She says I can't love somebody at my age because I don't know what it means. But I think I do. Isn't love when people are kind to each other? When they look after each other? I think that if Mum and Dad had been kinder to each other, Dad wouldn't have left.

She thinks about this. The bell rings.

Margie   I've got to go now. We've got Maths now and I've got to help Marcus with his fractions. But I don't mind. I love him.

She exits.

FORGETTING

Cast: *Jason, a twelve-year-old boy*
Mum
Dad
Jackie, Jason's older sister

Scene: *Jason's house. It is first thing in the morning.*
Everybody is rushing around.

Jason   My mum is always telling me not to forget.

Mum   Jason!!

Jason   Yes?!

Mum   Don't forget your football kit!

Jason   I won't! – See? She just doesn't trust me. I am
twelve years old and she doesn't trust me to
do anything!

Dad   Jason! Don't forget your English book! It's on top
of the telly where you left it last night! And I'M
not putting it in your bag for you, I can tell you
that NOW.

Mum   Jason! Have you remembered to eat your breakfast
yet? It'll be stone cold!

Jason   But it's cornflakes!

Mum   Never mind the cheek! Just don't forget to eat it or
there'll be no more. Buying food that's not being
eaten! I don't know why I bother, I really don't!

Jason   Okay! – My dad's just the same.

Dad   Who's forgotten to eat these cornflakes? It's just
waste. Maureen! Don't buy any more of these. He's
just forgotten to eat another bowl. They're all stuck
to the sides like cement!

Mum   I shan't, Frank, I can tell you. And have you
remembered to pay the electricity bill?

Dad   Er – yes.

Mum	Don't you lie to me. Well, when we get cut off, I'M not wasting my money on candles to burn the house down and leave us homeless, I can tell you! – Jason! Don't forget your dinner-money! What's it doing in your shoe?
Jason	It's in my shoe so that I'll remember it!
Mum	Well, make sure you do! I don't want the blame for you starving and having to be taken off to hospital and put on a drip for not taking your dinner-money with you.
Jason	See? I mean, what IS their problem? They treat me like a three-year-old. THEY'RE the ones who forget. I'M twelve. I'm practically a MAN!
Jackie	No, you're not. You're a flea, Flea-Man. So get out of my way before I tread on ya.
Jason	That's my sister, Jackie. I hate her. – I hate you!
Jackie	Yeah, right. I'm really frightened. I'm really frightened of someone whose nappy I used to help change when he was a little tiny baby. I haven't forgotten.
Jason	Oh, no! Not the embarrassing baby stories she always uses to win an argument with! – Shut up, you!
Jackie	AND I haven't forgotten how you used to run up to me every night before you went to bed for a big sloppy kiss off me either!
Jason	Shut up! I wouldn't do it now. I'd rather drink out of the toilet like the dog!
Dad	Jason!! Have you forgotten to give this dog a drink again? He's drinking out of the toilet! Get him out of here!
Jason	Soz, Dad! – (to Jackie) Later, Rat-Face!
Jackie	I don't think so, Flea-Man.
Jason	I'm just never going to get to school at this rate. – Come on, Dog. Out of there. And leave that toilet-roll alone! Who do you think you are? The Andrex Puppy? Go on, downstairs. Here's a drink for you.

Mum	Jason! Don't forget!
Jason	Oh, what now?!
Mum	Don't give him squash! He'll be in a terrible state like last time and I'M not cleaning it up!
Jason	All right, all right! – Tut! Too much to remember. Right. Football kit. English book. Given the dog a drink.
Jackie	Where's my face cream? I never forgot to buy some, did I? Have you had it, Flea-Man?
Jason	Oh, shut up! I'm trying to remember stuff. What would I want your face cream for?
Jackie	I don't know, do I? You're twelve. You're peculiar. You've probably taken my cream to make a spaceship out of or to do your Art homework with.
Jason	Don't talk stupid. You talk stupid, you do.
Jackie	You're looking for a kick in the pants, you are.
Jason	Oh, I'm really frightened, Rat-Face!
Jackie	You're not too old for one, so don't you forget.
Mum	Jackie! It's eight o'clock! You've got to get petrol!
Jackie	Oh, God! I forgot! See ya!
	Jackie exits.
Jason	Now, what was I doing? Oh, yes. Trying not to forget. Right. English book. Seen to the dog. Football kit. Dinner-money. That's it! Done it! Remembered everything! Ready for school! And they think I'm stupid. – I'm off now, Mum! See ya, Dad!
Mum	Good grief!
Jason	What now?!
Dad	Haven't you forgotten something, Son?
Jason	Like what?
Dad	Like you're still in your pyjamas.
Jason	Oh, no!!
Mum	And that means you've forgotten to have a wash! Get in that bathroom, Jason! This isn't my teaching, I can tell you that! He takes after you, Frank!

Dad	He looks like YOUR side of the family, though, Maureen!
Mum	Don't start on rubbish-talk like that at this time of the morning or we'll never get out of the house. Jason! Don't forget to use soap!
Jason	I KNOW!
Dad	You'd better take some up with you. There's none left in the bathroom.
Jason	Where is it?
Mum	Under the kitchen sink, Jason, where it always is! For goodness' sake!
Jason	Well, I can't see any. Where?
Mum	Behind the scouring pads.
Jason	There's none there!
Mum	Oh, get out of the way. I'll do it myself. – Oh.
Dad	What?
Mum	There's no soap left.
Jason	Thank you!
Mum	I must have forgotten to get some more. And is it a wonder? Having to remember everything for you lot!
Jason	Every morning! – Tell me – is it like this for you?

BULLIES

Cast: *Stryk*
Kuff
Grynd
Boot

Scene: *The street. Four bullies waiting for a bus.*

Stryk	It'll be good when the bus gets here.
Kuff	Really good.
Grynd	'Cause then we'll have something to do.
Boot	Like messing about.
Stryk	And having a laugh.
Kuff	And it'll be really funny.
Grynd	They've got cameras on the bus.
Boot	But we're not bothered.
Stryk	We'll try and smash them.
Kuff	Or throw something over them.
Grynd	But we'll do our stuff anyway.
Boot	And it'll be really good.
Stryk	Really funny.
Kuff	I'm gonna get that little kid with the red hair.
Grynd	The one with the glasses and the tatty sports bag.
Boot	And I'll take his glasses.
Stryk	'Cause he can't see without them.
Kuff	And then I'll take his bag off him.
Grynd	And get everything out.
Boot	And chuck it around everywhere.
Stryk	And then I'll stick the empty bag back on his head.
Kuff	And then I'll hit him.
Grynd	And then it'll be ever so funny.
Boot	'Cause when I take the bag off his head.

Stryk	He'll be crying.
Kuff	Like a girl.
Grynd	All snotty and red-eyed.
Boot	And that's when I'll give him back his glasses.
Stryk	After breaking them first, of course.
Kuff	Of course.
Grynd	When we've done that we'll laugh.
Boot	Very loud.
Stryk	So that everyone looks at us.
Kuff	'Cause it's great when people look at you.
Grynd	It makes you feel really important.
Boot	And strong.
Stryk	Powerful.
Kuff	The four of us together.
Grynd	People watch us all the time.
Boot	Spitting on the pavement.
Stryk	On the ceiling.
Kuff	On the windows.
Grynd	Pushing little kids around.
Boot	Pushing people out of the way.
Stryk	Swearing.
Kuff	Threatening.
Grynd	Hanging around.
Boot	Putting graffiti everywhere.
Stryk	Everywhere.
Kuff	Spray.
Grynd	Pen.
Boot	Brush.
Stryk	Stryk rules!
Kuff	Everyone gets a Kuff!
Grynd	Grynd them into the dirt!
Boot	Stick the Boot in!
Stryk	At school we're the same.

Kuff	Sticking together.
Grynd	Being strong.
Boot	Showing them just WHO we are.
Stryk	Striking!
Kuff	Cuffing!
Grynd	Grinding!
Boot	Booting!
Stryk	And when the teachers see us –
Kuff	We run off!
Grynd	Or say 'It wasn't us, Sir!'
Boot	'It was this little kid here, Miss.'
Stryk	'He was cheeking us, Sir.'
Kuff	'He said something about me mum.'
Grynd	'Me dad.'
Boot	'Me family.'
Stryk	Yeah!
Kuff	Take HIS side!
Grynd	As usual!
Boot	Not fair!
Stryk	I'm going home!
Kuff	I'm not staying here!
Grynd	I'm gonna tell me mum.
Boot	I'm gonna bring me dad up here.
Stryk	This place stinks!
Kuff	You teachers all stick together!
Grynd	You've got no right to suspend me!
Boot	You're just picking on me!
Stryk	You hate me!
Kuff	I'm telling!
Grynd	You can't shout at me and get away with it.
Boot	I'm important, I am!
Stryk	All the kids in my class are looking.
Kuff	I hate you!

Grynd	All the kids in my class are talking about me.
Boot	I hate you!
Stryk	I'll get me own back.
Kuff	When WE'RE back at school.
Grynd	Together!
Boot	And WE'LL graffiti!
Stryk	Together!
Kuff	And WE'LL push little kids around!
Grynd	Together!
Boot	And you'll wish you'd never bullied US!
Stryk	Stryk!
Kuff	Kuff!
Grynd	Grynd!
Boot	Boot!
All	Stryk! Kuff! Grynd! Boot! TOGETHER!

FAULT

Cast: *Cal*
Maz

Scene: *Two pupils outside the Headteacher's office.*

Cal It's not my fault.

Maz It's not mine.

Cal I'm not taking the blame.

Maz Neither am I.
Silence.

Cal I'm bringing my dad up if she starts on me.

Maz My nan'll go berserk.

Cal Because it's not our fault?

Maz Because I was smoking.
Silence.

Cal Wimp.

Maz Who is?

Cal You're frightened, aren't you?

Maz Me? No.

Cal You are. You're shaking.

Maz I'm cold.

Cal Look, it's not our fault. We're not to blame.

Maz We were smoking. By the sports shed.

Cal So? I'll take the blame for that. But not the rest.

Maz I can't help it . . .

Cal What?

Maz Feeling guilty.

Cal Well, DON'T!! That's what they're waiting to hear!
Then they'll drop the lot on you!

Maz I can't help it! That kid! Is he all right?

Cal I don't know, do I?

Maz He's only Year 7!

Cal Just shut up, will you? Who asked him to be there?

Maz What was he doing there? The shed's our place. The little kids shouldn't be there.

Cal They were playing some stupid game of Tracker or something – I don't know. He shouldn't have been there, should he?

Maz You keep saying that, but he was – and now he's in hospital.

Silence.

Maz Why were we messing about with lighters and cans?

Cal It wasn't my idea. It was Dag's. I'm not having that dumped on me.

Maz We might have known something would happen.

Cal What's all this 'we' stuff? When you go in there, you're on your own. I've got my story ready. I was having a smoke. Dag brought the cans. She made me set light to the sprays for a laugh. It's her fault that the kid got hurt.

Maz I never saw him come running round the corner of the shed. I was just aiming the flame at that dead tree. I never saw him! I didn't!

Cal Just get your story straight, Maz. 'Cause they're not going to be listening to that.

Silence.

Maz Straight in his face. The flame went straight in his face.

Silence.

Cal Are you blaming me?

Maz No.

Cal 'Cause I'm telling you now, if you blame me, I'll make sure you get the lot thrown at you.

Silence.

Maz He might lose his sight. His skin.

Silence.

Maz   We shouldn't have been smoking. Then it wouldn't have happened.

Cal   It wasn't us! It was Dag! Dag brought the cans!

Maz   We joined in! The responsibility was ours!

Cal   Responsibility?! You sound like a teacher. Listen – you go in there and tell the Head it was your fault. You were just having a smoke, but if you want to be a martyr –

Maz   I shouldn't have been.

Cal   I am NOT getting expelled for having a SMOKE!!! Do you hear me?!

Maz   I can hear that kid screaming! Even now!

Silence.

Cal   It's not my fault.

Silence.

Cal   I'm not taking the blame.

Silence.

Maz   I am. I have to.

PUMPKIN

Cast: *Pumpkin*

Scene: *A pumpkin is sitting on a chair next to a table. It is having a think. On the table is a newspaper.*

Pumpkin   Funny how life changes . . . One minute you're one thing – the next, you're another. All your dreams are suddenly – different.

The pumpkin looks up at the audience and speaks directly to them.

I don't remember being a seed. I suppose I was one once. Pushed into the ground by some farmer. Watered, then left to grow.

The pumpkin walks around the table, arms folded, deep in thought over the next few lines.

I DO remember being a young pumpkin. I was very green then. Very pale. Not luscious and orange like I am now. No – THEN I was just hard and sad and green all the way through. Sitting in the dirt with all the other hard, sad and green would-be pumpkins. Sitting there in the garden of the big house. The rain raining on me. The wind blowing on me. Waiting to get ripe.

It sits on the table as it remembers more.

And I did. I did get ripe. The other pumpkins were nothing compared to me! I was full, I was round, I was orange, I was – well, a pumpkin really. And what was my dream? To be picked first. To be carried into the big house and be made into rich people's soup! Not much of a dream, but a pretty basic ambition for your average pumpkin. Better than sitting in the dirt, anyway.

The pumpkin braces itself against the table with excitement.

And then – something WONDERFUL happened! There I was, one evening, minding my own business, when this girl came along. Very pretty she was, too. Not as good-looking as me, of course, but then, she WAS human. And a bit scruffy, I thought. Her dress was all ragged and her hair could have done with a comb through it. Anyway, she came straight up to me, snipped me from my stem and took me into the big house! I was so proud! The other pumpkins were green with envy – well, orange actually, but you know what I mean. I thought to myself, this is it. I'm for the soup! But no!

The pumpkin leans forward, its voice becoming more mysterious.

In the kitchen, there was this old woman. 'That one'll do nicely!' she said, looking at me as if I'd just won the prize of 'Pumpkin of The Year'. The next thing I knew, I'd been whisked back out into the garden. Were they going to have a picnic, I wondered? No. The girl put me on the ground very carefully next to these mice. I was astonished. They were never going to feed me to some mice?! The indignity of it all! A great pumpkin like me to end its days as fast-food for vermin! But then the old lady started babbling! All these words that didn't make sense – AND waving a stick about while she was saying them like a mad thing! Then – WHOOSH! – There was a cloud of stars and . . . I was a COACH!! An actual coach with wheels and everything! No flesh or juice – just glitter and gold!

The pumpkin leans back, very proud of itself.

Then we went to a party. At the palace, thank you very much. Me, the girl and the mice. The girl wasn't scruffy any more and had on this beautiful gown. The mice had turned into a team of horses – which is a good trick if you can do it. Unfortunately, the party can't have been any good as the girl left early. She was in quite a rush, too, legging it down the steps as the clock started to chime midnight. She was in such a state, she even left behind one of her slippers. Shame. It was a nice one, too. Glass. Quite difficult to get another one of those, I would have thought.

The pumpkin slowly sits up straight as it tells the final part of its story.

But within seconds, that cloud of stars was back and so was the girl's scruffy appearance. There we all sat at the side of the road, the mice scampering, a little dazed, over my thick skin and the girl – weeping. And then they all left me. Alone. I thought that was it. The next horse-and-cart that came along and – SPLAT! That would be the end of me. Not even a bowl of rich people's soup for my ending. Just a sloppy mess in the gutter.

The pumpkin stands up and takes a little step towards the audience.

But then, the strangest thing happened. I noticed that the cloud of stars had left a few behind – and they were sparkling at my feet. Feet? Where had they come from? In fact, where had these arms and legs come from?

It waggles its arms and legs at the audience.

And – I could read! Look!

It picks up the newspaper from the table and gives it a quick scan.

Because of the stars, I had not completely changed back. But – I HAD changed! In fact, my whole life has now changed because I can read and move about and think. Reading is brilliant. Rich people's soup? That's not good enough for me now! I've started teaching the others round here to read, too, and now we read the papers a lot. The business section mostly – grain prices, the cheese market – stuff like that. We're thinking of getting into the stock market. We're also thinking of starting up our own business, too. A coach firm. And all because we can read and understand now. Life couldn't be better.

The pumpkin listens to a question from someone in the audience.

That girl? Oh. She married some chap she'd met at the party. He found her glass slipper and tracked her down with it. Mind you, the coach she used for her wedding wasn't a patch on me when I was a coach. Still, she's not a poor, ragged creature with no future any more. That cloud again, you see. Funny how life changes. You just need a few stars . . .

POCKET-MONEY

Cast: *Kaz, a teenage girl*
            Mum
            Dad
            Tez, Kaz's older brother
            Cynth, Tez's twin sister
            Nan

Scene: *Kaz's house. Friday evening. It's Pocket-money Night!*

Kaz   Friday Night is Pocket-money Night! I can't wait! Here comes Mum. Carrying the pocket-money with her. The very money that will go towards the CD, the new trainers, the groovy jeans – or even the Kiss-Me-Quick lipstick-and-sexy-perfume set for the benefit of that lad in my Science class. This is it. The money. I hold out my eager hand!

Mum   There you go, Kaz. Your pocket-money.

Kaz   Thanks, Mum! (*looks at money*) A pound?

Mum   That's right.

Kaz   One pound?!

Mum   Don't spend it all at once.

Kaz   But –

Dad   Out the way, Kaz.

Kaz   But –

Dad   You're standing in front of the telly.

Kaz   BUT!

Dad   But what?

Kaz   But I can't exist on one pound a week!

Dad   Too bad. That's all you're getting.

Kaz   Wait a second. Maybe I counted it wrong. (*looks at hand*) One. – No. It's still only a quid. Why is it only a quid?

Mum	We have more to think about than your pocket-money, you know, Kaz. There's bills to pay.
Dad	Electricity.
Mum	Gas.
Dad	Water.
Mum	Plus the Council Tax.
Dad	And the shopping.
Kaz	But I wanted to get that CD. And the jeans! The jeans!
Mum	You know your trouble, Kaz? You're spoilt.
Dad	Spoilt.
Mum	You've had too much given to you.
Dad	Far too much. Now go and put the kettle on.
Kaz	(*hopefully*) For money?
Dad	For a cup of tea!
Kaz	But – if I do more round the house – will you pay me?
Dad	(*amused*) You?
Mum	(*even more amused*) Do more round the house?
Dad	You can't even make your bed properly!
Mum	You can't even put your knickers in the laundry basket!
Kaz	I can!
Mum	You miss!
Kaz	I don't!
Mum	Kaz, the bath is NOT the laundry basket. Never has been. Never will be.
Kaz	I could do the garden.
Dad	You are NOT wrecking my garden like last time. Fairy Liquid in the pond!
Kaz	I was trying to clean it out.
Dad	The fish were blowing bubbles like hot-air balloons!
	Tez walks in.
Tez	Who's going up in a hot-air balloon?

Mum	Oh. You're out of the bathroom at last, then, Tez?
Tez	It IS Friday night, isn't it?
Dad	It is.
Tez	Then Friday night is Debbie-Night and she likes me very clean and very smooth-shaven. Extra half-hour in the bathroom. Goes without saying.
Dad	Other people want to use that bathroom, you know. I've got a darts match on.
Tez	It'll be a bit crowded in there for a darts match, Dad. You'll have to take the sink out.
Dad	My son's a comedian.
Tez	So, who's going up in a hot-air balloon, then?
	Cynth wanders in.
Cynth	YOU ought to from the smell of you! Is that cheap after-shave, Terence, or are you dabbing Toilet-Duck behind your ears?
Tez	Ah, the lovely Cynthia! Are those false eyelashes, or have you glued a couple of dead spiders to your lids?
Cynth	Going out with Deadly Debbie? Or Vampira as she's known to her friends.
Tez	Going out with Drippy Dennis? Or Fish-Face as he's known to local anglers.
Cynth	He's a better man than you'll ever be.
Tez	YOU'RE a better man than he'll ever be!
Cynth	In your ear, Tez! Dad, can I have an advance on next week's money, please?
Tez	And me, please, Dad. I'm a bit strapped for cash.
Dad	No.
Cynth **Tez** }	Thanks. – No?!
Cynth	But I'm going out!
Tez	And I am!
Cynth **Tez** }	Mum?!
Mum	No!

Cynth	But I can't go out without any money!
Tez	Yeah. Debbie wants two lots of chips buying on a Friday!
Cynth	Oo! She's so exotic, that Debbie!
Mum	Well, she'll have to do without.
Tez	She won't do without!
Kaz	Who cares? If they're getting an advance, I want one as well.
Dad	They're not getting an advance.
Cynth	Keep out of this, Kaz! We're sixteen. We outrank you when it comes to getting an advance.
Mum	You're not getting an advance!
Kaz	Twins always stick together!
	Nan walks in.
Nan	What's all this arguing?
Cynth **Tez** **Kaz**	Nan!!
Cynth	I saw her first!
Tez	Get to the back of the queue, Kaz.
Kaz	That's not fair!
Nan	I can hear you lot in the street. What's happened?
Mum	Take no notice of any of them, Mum.
Tez	Nan, I need chip-money.
Cynth	Nan, I need club-money.
Kaz	Nan, I need lipstick-and-perfume-money at the very least!
Dad	They're on the scrounge for extra pocket-money because they've spent all theirs.
Nan	All three of my grandchildren need money? Sounds too good to be true.
Tez	You mean you'll give us the money?
Nan	I certainly will.
Cynth	Oh, Nan! You are so fabulous! I'd do anything for you!

Nan	You certainly will. You're going to be painting my back bedroom tomorrow.
Cynth	Tomorrow? But tomorrow's Saturday! I was going shopping tomorrow.
Nan	What with?
Tez	Oh, dear, Cynth! What a shame!
Nan	And you, Terence, are mowing my lawn and fixing the back fence.
Tez	But I was going out with Debbie tomorrow. Skating.
Nan	What with?! I'm sorry, why do these kids keep telling me they're going out when they know quite well that they cannot do so without MY money. And they cannot have MY money without doing MY jobs. Now is that clear? Ten o'clock tomorrow morning. The both of you. My house.
Cynth Tez	(sulkily) Yes, Nan.
Kaz	What would you like ME to do for you, Nan?
Nan	You can fix the stuff you broke last time you needed an advance.
Kaz	No problem.
Nan	That's settled, then. And here's your advance. Now, off you go.
Tez	Come on, Cynth. I'll walk you to the fish shop.
Cynth	I'm not going to the fish shop.
Tez	But I thought you were meeting Dennis.
Cynth	Don't start with the fish jokes again, thank you. They're not funny.
Tez	He's got a three-second memory like a goldfish. – 'Hello, Cynthia. Lovely to see you. Let's go to the . . . Why, Cynthia! What are YOU doing here?'
Cynth	Yeah. Just don't forget Debbie's blood-bag selection.
	Tez and Cynthia leave.
Mum	Thank goodness they've gone for five minutes! Money! That's all they ever seem to want.

Dad	I'm off now, love. Er – you couldn't lend me a fiver, could you? Just to be on the safe side. I've overspent this week.
Mum	Scrounger!
Dad	I'll do the same for you tomorrow when you go out with the girls!
Mum	You'd better!
Nan	You're as bad as the kids!
Kaz	I could lend you a quid, but don't ask for any more.
Mum **Dad** }	Get to your room!
Kaz	Tut! Parents!

ORDER

Cast: *Mum*
Clare
Den
Dad
Barry
Waitress

Scene: *A restaurant. The family is about to order.*

Mum	Well, this is very nice, isn't it?
Clare	I wanted to go to Burger Empire.
Den	Here we go!
Clare	Oh, shut it, Den.
Den	Can't eat anything unless she can pick it up with her hands.
Dad	Not in a restaurant, thank you.
Den	Like a rusk.
Clare	Dad! He's picking on me again!
Dad	Don't you two DARE start rowing in here. Look, Marie, perhaps we should eat at Burger Empire. I don't want these two having a fight.
Den	Dad, I would never start a fight in a restaurant with my twelve-year-old sister.
Dad	Good man.
Den	I am a sophisticated teenager now.
Clare	Yeah, right. Fifteen's sophisticated.
Den	And as such I am quite happy to be in a sophisticated restaurant.
Mum	Which is as it should be.
Den	However, Clare is still a cave-animal and cannot cope with cutlery.
Clare	I can!

Den	What's cutlery then?
Clare	Knives and forks!
Den	Oh! I'm impressed. You're getting better, Rock-Head.
Clare	Mum!
Mum	That's enough, Den! Can't we go anywhere without you two having a scrap?
Dad	Behave yourselves, the both of you!
Barry	(*looking at menu*) I want the tomato soup.
Dad	There. See? Your baby brother knows how to behave at the table and he's only five!
Clare	Yeah, but he's reading the menu upside-down.
Den	You noticed, Clare! Another major step forward!
Barry	And chips.
Mum	There's a good boy! See? Barry knows exactly what he wants ready for when the waitress comes over. Unlike you two! – Who's a good boy, then, Barry? Who's Mummy's cleverest little love?
Den	Not Clare, that's for sure.
Clare	Dad!
Dad	You two wait till we get home!
Den	It's not me! It's her!
Dad	Shut up! The waitress is here!
Waitress	Good evening. I'm Shirley. I'll be your waitress for this evening. Are you ready to order?
Mum	Yes, certainly.
Barry	I want the tomato soup. And chips.
Mum	Just a minute, darling. Mummy and Daddy first.
Dad	I'll have the –
Mum	Derek!
Dad	Sorry, Marie. After you. (*to Waitress, trying to make a joke of it*) The missus first, eh?
Mum	Derek!
Dad	Joke! Just a joke.
Den	Just.

Mum	I'll have the melon balls to start with, then the lemon chicken.
Waitress	Fries, stir-fry or jacket potato with that, Madam?
Mum	Oh. Er – gosh! The fries sound really nice, don't they?
Clare	(*knowing this next bit*) But I AM dieting.
Mum	But I AM dieting. So – jacket potato, then.
Waitress	Vegetables or salad, Madam?
Mum	Oh. Er – gosh! Er –
Clare	Salad.
Mum	Thank you, Clare. I CAN order my own meal, you know. (*to Waitress*) Children. They're so cheeky, aren't they?
Clare	But you always have salad. Always.
Barry	I want the tomato soup.
Mum	Just a minute, Barry! – Perhaps I will have the stir-fry. (*to Waitress*) Is the stir-fry cooked in vegetable or olive oil?
Clare	Oh, man!
Waitress	Lard, probably. Wouldn't know, to be honest, Madam. I'll ask Chef.
Mum	Oh, not to worry. I'll stick to the jacket potato. Er – and I'll have the salad.
Clare	Told you.
Waitress	(*to Dad*) And for you, Sir?
Dad	Sir? Oo, I like it when a woman calls me 'Sir'.
Mum	Derek!
Dad	Just a joke!
Clare	Just.
Dad	I'll have the deep-fried mushrooms and garlic bread for starters, please.
Clare ⎱ **Den** ⎰	What? Oh, no! Mum!
Mum	I don't think so, dearest. What about the egg mayonnaise?
Dad	I don't want the egg mayonnaise!

Barry	I want the tomato soup.
Dad	Just a minute, Barry. Daddy's fighting for his rights here. – Marie, I'm having the mushrooms.
Clare **Den** }	But, Dad!!
Dad	And you two can stay out of it.
Clare	But, Dad – they make you –
Mum	Clare!!
Den	They give you wind, Father. For once I agree with Clare.
Clare	Dad, the only way you could eat mushrooms and not take off is if you swallowed some blotting-paper with them.
Den	Or soaked them in Milk of Magnesia.
Dad	All right, all right! I'll have the egg mayonnaise. God!
Waitress	And for your main course, Sir?
Dad	(*sarcastically*) Well, I don't know. You'd better ask THEM.
Mum	Derek, don't sulk in front of the waitress, please.
Dad	(*sulking*) I'm not sulking.
Waitress	Main course, Sir?
Dad	I don't want one any more.
Barry	I'll have Daddy's tea AND the tomato soup.
Mum	(*to Waitress*) He'll have the same as me.
Den	I don't want a starter and then I'll have the Pasta Surprise.
Waitress	Is that with or without the surprise, Sir?
Den	Sorry?
Waitress	With or without the pasta, Sir?
Den	With, please.
Clare	I just want a burger.
Waitress	I'm sorry. We only do burgers on the children's menu.
Den	That's all right. (*picking up the children's menu*) Now then, Clare. Do we want a whale-burger with

	fishy-dishy chips, or do we want a clown-burger with happy-face chips?
Clare	Mum!
Mum	Could she have the burger with grown-up chips, please?
Waitress	I'll ask Chef. And for the little chap here?
Barry	I'll have tomato soup and Daddy's tea, please.
Mum	There's a good boy, Barry. He said 'please'. There's ever such a good boy, Barry.
Waitress	And the main course?
Barry	Daddy's tea.
Mum	No, no, Barry. Daddy's changed his mind. He's going to have his own tea now.
Dad	Says who?
Mum	Derek! Behave!
Dad	I'd just like to know – you and WHOSE army is going to make me, Marie, that's all?
Den	Oh, for goodness' sake, Father.
Dad	And I'll have less of the high-and-mighty stuff from you as well, young fella. I used to change your nappies.
Den	Dad!
Mum	Not as often as I did, Derek.
Den	Mum!
Waitress	Sorry. Could I ask you for the little boy's order, please? We close in five hours.
Mum	Sorry. Barry? Chips, wasn't it?
Barry	Yes.
Mum	And?
Barry	Cacky.
Mum **Dad** **Clare** **Den**	} Barry!!
Barry	But Daddy said it.

Dad   I never!

Mum   What did Daddy say, Barry?

Barry   Daddy said that he was going to have cacky for his tea here.

Den   (*realising the truth*) Did he now? And was he talking to Clare at the time, Barry?

Barry   Yes. And Daddy and Clare said that they'd rather go to Burger Empire because if they came here they'd have cacky for tea. Cacky for tea and a play-up. So I'll have cacky as well. But not a play-up because I'm a big boy now.

Silence.

Mum   Cacky, Derek?

Silence.

Waitress   I'll ask Chef.

FANS

Cast: *Kaz, a teenage girl*
        Shaz, a teenage girl
        Jaz, a teenage girl
        Tim, a teenage boy

Scene: *Four friends sitting in their form room. The girls are looking at teen magazines. Tim is reading a computer magazine.*

Kaz   He's lovely.

Shaz He's got lovely hair.

Jaz   Lovely eyes.

Kaz
Shaz } Ah!
Jaz

Tim   Are you three talking about me again?

Kaz
Shaz } No!
Jaz

Tim   Now you know you are really.

Kaz
Shaz } We're not!
Jaz

Tim   Well, who ARE you on about, then?

Shaz Dermot Devlin!

Jaz   From the band Celtic Nomads.

Tim   Oh. Him. He's rubbish.

Kaz   He is not!

Tim   He looks like a girl.

Shaz He does not!

Tim   He wears a dress!

Jaz   It's a kaftan, actually. It's ethnic.

40

Tim	You mean hippy. He's stupid. AND he can't sing.
Kaz	I wish he'd walk into the room.
Shaz	I wish he'd walk into the room right now.
Jaz	I wish he'd walk into the room right now – and I'd – and I'd scream.
Kaz **Shaz**	Oo, and I would!
Tim	What for?
Kaz	Because he's lovely.
Shaz	You just don't understand, Tim. Read your computer magazine.
Jaz	Yeah. All those hard-drives and mega-nothings.
Tim	There's more point to this than what you do.
Jaz	There isn't!
Tim	There is. At least I can look at these pictures and buy something. You can't look at a picture of Dermot Drill-Head and buy him, can you?
Kaz	Oo!
Shaz	Buy Dermot Devlin!
Jaz	Oo! You've started me off again now!
Kaz	I'd pay anything.
Tim	But you can't! That's the point. You can't buy him.
Jaz	We can buy his music.
Shaz	And videos.
Kaz	Did you see his latest one?
Shaz	With him in the boat?
Jaz	Sailing towards that woman with the flowers in her hair?
Kaz	And the stars above their heads.
Shaz	And the breeze flowing softly across the canal.
Jaz	And he moves that oil-drum out of the way and that big bag of rubbish so that he can get to her.
Kaz	He's so strong!

Shaz	He's so romantic!
Jaz	And singing to her at the same time!
Kaz **Shaz** **Jaz**	Wow!
Tim	I feel ill.
Kaz	Oh, shut up.
Shaz	Have you heard his latest song?
Jaz	Oh, you mean 'Siren Dream'?
Shaz	No, no, that was his last one.
Kaz	Oh, I know the one! 'Tidal Wave Sensation'?
Shaz	No! That's the CD album. I mean his very latest, 'Flowing From The Heart'.
Kaz	Oh, yeah! I've heard that one! It's ever so romantic.
Tim	Got a water fixation, hasn't he? Is that because he's a big drip? You do waste your money on that sad singer.
Jaz	He's not a sad singer! He's THE BUSINESS!
Tim	It's such a shame.
Kaz	What is?
Tim	You're just pitiful and totally obsessed.
Shaz	Let's have a look at YOUR magazine, then.
Tim	Give us that back!
Kaz	Yeah. Let's see how wonderful it is. Two pounds fifty?! Oh, you do waste your money on this sad computer stuff!
Tim	It's not sad! A madman singer in a dress singing a song about jump-leads to his girlfriend whilst sitting on an oil-drum! Now THAT'S sad!
Jaz	Look at this! Page 14! Wow! New games!
Kaz	'Deadliest Mortality Blood-Spurt Revenge'? What kind of game's that?
Tim	A really good one.
Shaz	About what?
Tim	Gardening! What do you think?

Jaz	What do you have to do?
Tim	I'm not telling you.
Jaz	Why not?
Tim	'Cause you'll make fun of me, that's why not.
Kaz	Now why should we make fun of your very serious computer magazine just because you've ripped our beloved Dermot to pieces?
Shaz	We wouldn't do that, would we?
Jaz	Certainly not. We're mature.
Kaz	So go on, Tim. Reveal all.
Tim	All right, but you'd better not make fun of it 'cause it's really serious.
Jaz	We won't.
Tim	Well – There's two gangs – The Bloods and The Spurts – and you get to be in one of the gangs and fight the other one.
Kaz **Shaz** **Jaz**	What a load of rubbish!
Tim	I knew it! Shut up!
Kaz	Sounds really boring.
Tim	Boring?! It's brilliant! I've got the whole series.
Shaz	Series? There's more of them?
Tim	Yeah! There's 'Deadliest Mortality Blood-Spurt Revenge: The Beginning' followed by 'Deadliest Mortality Blood-Spurt Revenge: The Battle' followed by 'D.M.B-S.R.: The Hospitalization' followed by –
Jaz	Oh, don't tell me any more!
Kaz	How dreary!
Tim	I'm getting the next one for my birthday! I live to load up! You should see all the stuff I've got. And the posters! And what I really want is a virtual-reality set-up where I can really INTERACT with the gangs! Really do THE BUSINESS!
	Pause.

Kaz	Shame, isn't it?
Shaz	Yeah. Pitiful.
Kaz	He's just totally obsessed.
Tim	Look who's talking!
Kaz	Look out. Teacher's coming.
Shaz	She'll be in here with her *X-Files* magazine again.
Jaz	She's on about that stuff all the time.
Tim	Was Shakespeare an alien?
Kaz	Did Wordsworth have a Close Encounter whilst looking at those daffodils?
Shaz	Now she IS obsessed.

Kaz
Shaz
Jaz   } She's such a fanatic!
Tim

AWAY

Cast: *Liz, a teenage girl*
         Abby, a teenage girl
         Ali, a teenage girl
         Beast, a teenage boy
         Gob, a teenage boy
         Woof, a teenage boy

Scene One: *The girls' dormitory of an educational
            residential centre. The girls are
            lounging about the place.*

Liz   This is brilliant! Away from home! No more sharing
       for a week!

Abby   Do you share?

Liz   With my kid sister. It's like sharing with a gorilla. I've
       asked Mum if she can live in the dog's basket with
       him, but she said no.

Ali   I don't like it here.

Abby   Why not? Staying in a converted stately home in the
       middle of the countryside? I do! It's fab!

Liz   It's a lovely place. Great big views. Great big
       staircases. Great big paintings on the walls.

Ali   I got puffed out walking up those stairs. And those
       paintings are staring at me.

Liz   All of them?

Ali   Yes.

Liz   Including the one of the sheep?

Ali   Especially the one of the sheep. I bet this place is
       haunted. I'll never sleep.

Liz   Well, I like it here. Five days of doing Music, Art and
       Drama. No kid sister. No workmen.

Abby   Still digging up the road outside your house, are
       they?

Liz	Sewage pipe being fixed. Terrible stink and a load of blokes reading the paper.
Ali	This place stinks of cow poo. I'd rather have the sewage pipe.
Abby	Oh, Ali!
Ali	And I like my own bed. This is all lumpy. And the trees and grass give me hay-fever.
Liz	But apart from that, you're delighted to be here. – What are you doing, Abby?
Abby	I've brought my own food with me.
Liz	Why? We get fed here.
Abby	That horrible muck? I wouldn't give it to the dog.
Liz	You had two helpings of apple crumble just now!
Abby	That was only because I couldn't believe how bad it was the first time.
Ali	It was probably poisoned. With cow poo.
Liz	Why am I stuck in a dorm with you two?
Ali	What've you got to eat, Abby?
Abby	Enough chocolate for the week. Five packets of biscuits. Ten yoghurts. Fresh fruit. Tinned fruit.
Liz	TINNED fruit?
Abby	For breakfast. Or for mashing up as a face-pack.
Ali	Isn't that bananas?
Abby	Isn't what bananas?
Ali	You mash bananas up for a face-pack. Not tinned fruit.
Abby	Oh. So NOW what am I going to do with all these tins of cling peaches?
Liz	You could stun yourself with them.
Abby	Not very helpful, Liz. As usual.
Liz	Let's change the subject. What are you doing this afternoon for your first class?
Abby	Drama. They're doing improvisation based on ecology and being close to nature.
Ali	Oh. Cow poo again.

Liz   Must everything you say come back to cow poo, Ali?

Ali   All right, all right. I'm doing Art this afternoon. Exploring with earth colours.

Liz   Like brown.

Ali   I am not saying cow poo. You are trying to make me say it, but I am not going to.

Liz   I'm doing a drum workshop in Music.

Abby   Oh. A lot of the boys are doing that.

Ali   Mmm. Yes. Well, I wonder why Liz is doing it then?

Abby   Can't imagine.

Liz   Don't start.

Ali   Beast wouldn't happen to be taking the workshop, would he?

Liz   I do not fancy Beast.

Abby   You know, I hear he is. Because drumming gives Beast the excuse to make even more noise than he already does.

Liz   He's not noisy. He's just – expressive.

Ali   Expressive! Oh, I see. Setting off the fire alarm as soon as we got here was very expressive, wasn't it?

Liz   It wasn't Beast. It was Gob.

Abby   Gob hasn't got the brains to set off a fire alarm. He couldn't break the glass without an instruction manual.

Ali   Not like Woof.

Abby   Woof? Oh, now you're talking! A real man!

Ali   I can see why Woof would want to do the drum workshop. Because all that drumming is just like the sound he makes when he's wagging his tail.

Abby   When he's happy!

Ali   After he's been a clever dog for Beast!

Liz   Are you saying that Beast treats his friends like dogs?

Ali
Abby }   Er – yes!

Liz   I like Beast. He's a rebel.

Ali	He's a pebble.
Abby	His brain is.
	Beast and Gob enter.
Beast	Did I hear my name mentioned?
Gob	I think you did, Beastie-Boy. I think the chicks were talking about you.
Liz	Don't call me a chick, Gob, or I'll smash your face in!
Gob	(*frightened of her*) Oh. Okay, then.
Abby	Who asked you to come in here? Oy! Get off my bed, Beast!
Beast	Hey! This isn't fair. This bed's softer than mine. Oy! Woof! Make a note of this!
Ali	Oh, don't bring him in here!
	Enter Woof.
Woof	Yes, Beast? Did you want something?
Beast	Get your notebook out. I want to make a complaint to give to Timpson.
Abby	MISTER Timpson to you, BERNARD.
Beast	That's BEAST, Abby. Beast. Don't call me Bernard, OKAY?!
Abby	Ooo! Touchy, touchy!
Woof	(*notebook in hand*) What do you want me to write down, Beast?
Beast	Take dictation. Er – 'Listen here, Timpson. We want softer beds like the girls have got or there'll be trouble. Okay? Plus, get the painting of the gloomy old bag out of our dorm, too.'
Woof	(*scribbling*) Okay. Got that, Beast.
Gob	Oh, yeah. Her. The old hag who used to live here. Hundred years ago, wasn't it, Beast?
Beast	Hundred and fifty.
Gob	Oh, yeah. Right. You're right, Beast.
Beast	I always am, Gob, me boy. Yeah, make a note about that painting. She's – challenging my authority.

Abby She's frightening you, you mean.

Beast Nothing frightens me, Babe.

Abby I'm not your babe, BERNARD.

Beast Watch it. You're stepping close to the point of no return.

Abby Tremble, tremble.

Woof I'll hand this in to Timpson, shall I, Beast? Or do you want to do it?

Liz He'll stick you in detention until you rot.

Abby He's not going to hand that to Timpson, Liz.

Beast I am. I mean what I say and I do what I do.

Ali Philosophy! Wow!

Gob Don't you mean, you mean what you do and say what you feel?

Woof Or even, you feel that what you do you should SAY, but you don't feel like it?

Beast Gentlemen?

Gob
Woof } Yes?

Beast Shut it.

Abby You're putrid, you are, Beast. You talk to people like scum.

Ali Yeah. Get out of our dorm!

Beast Oh! And who's going to make me, Ali-Cat?

Ali Me.

Beast You?! Go on, then. Try it, Moaner.

Ali Moaner?

Beast Yeah. That's what everybody calls you. Never happy anywhere. You don't like this. You don't like that.

Gob Yeah. You're really a moaner, you are. Everybody says so.

Beast And nobody likes you in our year. Not even your friends. Why don't you just go back to school and moan there?

Woof Shall I make a note of that, Beast?

Beast	Save your lead. Let's move on out of this sad nowhere place, gentlemen.
Gob	I'm right behind you, Beast. Shall we go and wreck the toilets or something?
Woof	We tried. We couldn't find them. Could we, Beast?
Beast	They must be behind some secret panel. I'll find them. Let's go.
Gob	Can I write rude things about other kids on the walls this time, Beast? Only Woof had the marker-pen last time and it's my go.
Beast	Marker-pen to you, Gob.
Gob	Thanks, Beast.
Beast	Make a note of that, Woof. Taking the drum workshop this afternoon, Liz?
Liz	Yeah.
Beast	I'll see you there then.
Liz	Yeah.

The boys leave.

Abby	Yeah?! How could you, Liz?!
Liz	How could I what?
Abby	Suck up to HIM?! He's a creep!
Liz	I was just answering his question. I WILL be seeing him at the drum workshop.
Abby	But what about what he's just said?! And why didn't you stick up for yourself, Ali? How could you just stand there and let him talk to you like that? – Ali? Ali, are you listening to me?

Pause.

Ali	I think this house is haunted.
Abby	What? Oh, don't start all that again!
Liz	I agree, Ali. I think it IS.
Abby	Not you as well!
Ali	Definitely haunted.
Liz	By the former lady of the house.

Ali	And I don't think she likes some of the naughty children running around her place at the moment.
Liz	Definitely not. I think she's going to appear to them.
Ali	And tell them off.
Liz	Definitely.
Abby	What are you two up to?
Ali	Nothing. I've just thought of something to do with those cling peaches.
Liz	Definitely.

End of Scene One

NOTE: If you would like to do the follow-up prediction activity on page 158, you should do this before reading Scene Two.

Scene Two: *The boys' dormitory that night.*

Gob	Are you all right now, Beast? Do you want some more water for your bandage?
Beast	Compress, Gob. It's called a cold compress, not a bandage. I'm not wounded.
Woof	That drum bouncing off your head brained you a bit though, didn't it, Beast?
Beast	I slipped and fell into the drum. It didn't bounce off my head.
Woof	Oh. Well, when I looked you had a drum on your head.
Beast	Woof?
Woof	Yes?
Beast	Take a message to yourself.
Woof	*(takes a notebook out)* What is it?
Beast	Shut it!
Woof	Oh. Okay.

Gob	You showed those chicks a thing or two this morning, eh, Beast?
Beast	Yeah. I did, didn't I?
Gob	Liz really fancies you.
Beast	Yeah. She does, doesn't she?
Gob	She rushed to help you when that drum bounced off your head – er – when you fell into that drum, I mean. Which was really smart 'cause everyone else was laughing at you.
Beast	Who was?!
Gob	Oh. Well – not laughing at you exactly, but – you know – finding it difficult not to show how – er – SHOCKED they were – by – er – accidentally – er – being amused by what happened. But in a SHOCKED way, obviously. Not laughing.
Woof	Funny how when she went to help you, you got poked in the eye with that drumstick, wasn't it? Is it feeling better now?
Beast	No.
Woof	Oh.
	Pause.
Gob	You know, maybe that inscription we found was right. The one written on the old parchment.
Beast	Oh, don't start on about that again, Gob!
Woof	No, don't. You'll frighten me.
Gob	Oh, shut up, Woof, you wus!
Woof	I'm not a wus. I've just got a very weak bladder.
Gob	'Beware ye who enter into this house with malice in your hearts' it said.
Beast	He's off!
Gob	'For unto him shall befall the terrible Curse Of The Giblets!' it said!
Woof	Oo! The Curse Of The Giblets. I don't like the sound of that. I mean, I don't know what they are, but I don't want them coming anywhere near me. I've got a weak bladder, I have. AND a dodgy knee.

Beast	Let's try that out, shall we?

He hits Woof in the knee.

Woof	Ow! Me knee!
Beast	Just shut up, then! Curse Of The Giblets! Behave!
Woof	But what ARE giblets?
Beast	Animals' insides! Heart, liver, kidneys – stuff like that. So, to be cursed by them probably means your insides get cursed – pain and torture and stuff like that. – Woof? – Woof, are you listening to me?
Woof	Hang on. I've just got to go to the lav.

Woof runs out of the room.

Gob	It certainly was an old parchment – all brown and burnt-looking with age. And a bit stinky, I thought. Like cow poo. Mind you, that's how you found it, isn't it, Beast? By the smell. Remember? When we brought you up here to lie down and you thought it was me.
Beast	Yeah.
Gob	And you sprayed me with your deodorant? What's it called again?
Beast	'Butch: For Men.'
Gob	That's it. But it was the parchment under your pillow, wasn't it? But who put it there? That's the question. I mean, it was signed Lady Georgina. But it can't have been her. 'Cause she's the lady in the painting over there on that wall. And she's dead.

Pause.

Gob	It gets really creepy out here in the country at night, doesn't it?

Pause.

Gob	I hope she doesn't haunt the place.
Beast	Will you shut up!!
Gob	Sorry, Beast. I didn't mean to frighten you. I forgot the old lady's painting scared you.
Beast	She does NOT frighten me! OKAY?!!

Pause.

Gob Sorry.

Beast It's just a painting, right? And this parchment is someone's idea of a joke. Now get into bed and go to sleep. You and Woof have been hopping around this room all on edge ever since the sun went down, cranking on about ghosts and curses and you wished you'd never set the fire alarm off or graffitied in the toilets! And you're getting up my NOSE!

Gob Sorry.

Beast There IS no ghost. There IS no curse. And I don't want to hear another word about it.

Woof (*rushing back in*) HELP!! HELP!! She's after me!!

He jumps on top of Gob.

Gob Ow!! Get off, Woof! You're squashing me, you great lump!

Woof Don't let her get me giblets! I'll never be naughty again!

Beast Calm down! What happened?

Woof I was just going to the lav when I saw something moving in the shadows at the end of the corridor! And it was a lady!

Gob And?

Woof And nothing! I legged it back here as quick as I could! It was terrifying! – And –

Beast Yes?

Woof Worst of all.

Gob Yes?

Woof I didn't get to go to the toilet! I'm absolutely busting for a wee!

Beast Oh, for goodness sake! Go, will you?

Woof What? Go back there? I'd rather wet myself!

Abby's voice is heard from off stage.

Abby (*very creepy*) Oooo!

Woof Agh! It's her! It's her!

Abby Wilfred? Wilfred Jenkins?

Gob	Woof! She knows your name!! Agh!
Abby	Wilfred Jenkins . . . You have disgraced my walls with obscene comments and caused havoc under my roof with your alarm bells!
Woof	It wasn't me! The alarm wasn't me! That was Gob! Take HIS giblets! I haven't got many to spare!
Gob	Woof, you rotten little grasser!
Abby	You, Wilfred Jenkins, have disturbed the spirit of this house and now revenge will be mine!
Woof	Please don't hurt me! You don't know how bad pain is for me!
Gob	Tell her about your bladder!
Woof	Yes! I've got a weak bladder! Please don't make me wet myself!
Abby	Then there is YOU, Gordon Blakesley!
Gob	She knows my name! Did you tell her, Woof?
Woof	I need the lav!
Abby	You, Gordon Blakesley, are a miserable sinner! A snivelling little yes-man! A sucker-upper!
Gob	Agh! She must have been talking to my mum!
Abby	DON'T deny it!
Gob	I'm not denying it! I'm not! I AM a rotten little snivelling little yes-man! With knobs on!
Abby	Then for this you must be punished. And for writing in the toilets that Hazel Pritchard is a spotty alien!
Gob	Beast made me write that! It was his fault! She wouldn't let him copy her Maths homework! He's always doing things like that! Isn't he, Woof?
Woof	Yes! And he treats me like a slave, keeping notes for him and ordering me about!
Gob **Woof** }	Give HIM The Curse Of The Giblets! Not us!!
Beast	You couple of creeps! You turn-coats! You – you splat-pants merchants!
Abby	And as for YOU, Bernard Sutton . . .!

Beast   Don't call me Bernard!

Abby   As for you, BERNARD – you are a wretched and vile nobody who has no right to even breathe the same air as the rest of the pupils on this residency! The greatest part of my curse will be upon YOU! You have nothing but contempt for everyone around you. Is that not TRUE?! SPEAK!

Gob
Woof   } It's true! It's true!

Beast   You don't frighten ME!

Abby   (*appearing as a figure in the doorway*) Don't I?!

Beast   Agh! It's her! It's the lady from the painting! She's horrible! She looks like me Auntie Wendy! The one who goes motor-biking with the Hell's Angels in Dorset! Help! Help! Save me! Save me!

Abby   Admit to all you have done! All the cruelty! All the breaking of rules!

Beast   I admit it! I admit it! Just don't come any nearer!

Abby   Apologise for all that you have done! For upsetting those nice girls this morning especially, you nasty little child!

Beast   I apologise! Don't curse me! I haven't been well today! I had a drum bounced off my head. And I nearly poked my eye out!

Abby   ENOUGH! Request denied! The Curse Of The Giblets is upon you all!!!!

Beast
Gob   } AGH! HELP!
Woof

Something pours down on them.

Gob   Urgh! Giblets raining down on us! It's horrible!

Woof   Sticky blood and stomachs slithering all down me!

Beast   It's all in my hair! In my eyes! I can't see! Get me away from this place! I'll never be naughty again! I promise!

Beast
Gob   } HELP!!
Woof

Suddenly the lights go on.

Liz And cut!

Abby Okay. That's a wrap. Okay on video, Ali?

Ali I got it all!

Abby Great! Can I get out of this dress now? It's got to go back to the Drama Department. And the camera.

Liz After we've shown it to the teachers.

Ali And the rest of the year-group.

Beast You three!! A set-up! I've been set up by three GIRLS!

Liz That's right! BERNARD!

Abby And you'd better get this room cleaned up before the teachers come.

Ali Yeah. Get all the giblets off the floor, BOYS!

The girls all walk out, laughing.

Woof (*eating the giblets*) Oh. Cling peaches.

Gob I like cling peaches.

Beast SHUT UP!

US

Cast: *Jay (male)*
Dee (female)
Em (female)
Bee (female)
Aitch (male)
Ex (male)

Scene: *An eating-area. Dinnertime. Jay, Dee and Em are eating together.*

Jay So I said, 'Try that again and you're dead meat.'

Dee And what did he say?

Jay I don't know. I ran away before he had time to say anything.

Em How come?

Jay He had fists the size of elephants' elbows. I wasn't going to mess with him.

Dee Jay – you're such a he-man.

Jay You think so? I knew you did. – What's that you're eating, anyway?

Dee Cheese and salad roll. Why? What's it to you?

Jay No. I mean the chips.

Em Oh, no. I feel either a calorie-count or a fat-gram estimate coming on.

Jay Do you know anything about cholesterol, Dee?

Em Oh. Cholesterol. New one.

Dee Cholesterol? Yeah. I know about cholesterol. Do you know about minding your own business?

Jay Eating chips is like greasing up your blood-vessels with lard.

He takes a chip.

Dee	Thank you, Doctor. Don't think that just because you've swallowed that chip that it's safe, because it isn't.
Jay	It isn't?
Dee	No.
Jay	No?
Dee	No. Because I could put my hand down your throat and drag it out again.
Jay	I'll bet.
Dee	But I won't. Because . . .
Em	You're kind.
Dee	I'm kind.
Em	Touching, isn't it?
Jay	I'm moved. Really. – (*sees Bee with her tray*) There's Bee. – Bee! Sit with us.
Bee	No.
Jay	Why not?
Em	She's fussy who she eats with.
Bee	I'm fussy who I eat with.
Em	It's okay, Bee. Jay's not eating spaghetti today.
Bee	I'll give it a shot then. Budge up.
	Bee sits down.
Jay	I like it when she says that.
Bee	Shut it, Dirt-Bag. – Guess what I heard?
Em	What?
Bee	The Great Love Affair is back on.
Em	The G.L.A. ? You're kidding!
Bee	I jest not.
Jay	Frankie Zane and Tracey Fenton? Can't be.
Dee	Not after last time.
Bee	It's back on, I tell you.
Jay	But he dumped her at the last disco in front of all her friends for Gail Price.
Bee	He said he was sorry.

Em	Tracey's SO forgiving.
Dee	Charitable, I'd call it. In a major dogs' home and sad cats' hospital kind of way.
Jay	I don't believe it.
Bee	Ask Aitch. – Aitch!
Aitch	(*coming over*) What? Don't shout. I've got a headache.
Jay	I'll have your chips then, Aitch. They're bad for headaches.
	Jay takes a chip.
Aitch	Put that back!
Jay	Just one! I'm saving your life.
	He eats the chip.
Aitch	Animal.
Bee	Sit down, Aitch.
Aitch	What?
	Aitch sits down.
Bee	What is back on?
Aitch	The G.L.A. Why?
Jay	Impossible!
Aitch	Eat your fish. It's good for you.
Jay	I hate fish without chips.
Aitch	Then why didn't you have chips with it?
Jay	Chips are bad for you.
Aitch	Cholesterol.
Jay	Right. See? Aitch knows. He understands me.
Em	Aitch has a double helping of cake plus synthetic whipped cream on his tray.
Aitch	I'm a growing boy.
Em	Yeah. Sideways.
Aitch	Funny. Em, you're funny.
Ex	(*joining them, sitting down immediately*) Never fear. I am here.
All	Go away, Ex!

Ex	You don't mean that.
Dee	You owe me a quid, Ex.
Em	And me, Ex.
Ex	And you'll get it back.
Dee	When?
Em	Soon-when or later-when?
Ex	Tomorrow-when.
Em	I won't hold my breath.
Dee	I want mine now.
Ex	You can't.
Dee	Why not?
Ex	I've spent it.
Dee	On what?
Ex	On these chips.
Em	Did ANYBODY not have chips?
Jay	I didn't.
Dee	We are so unhealthy.
Em	We ought to jog or something.
Jay	I jog.
Aitch	You do not.
Jay	I do, then.
Aitch	When?
Jay	Every day. To the lav.
Ex	That doesn't count.
Jay	Oh, yes, it does! There's a lot of stairs to the lav in this school. You daren't get caught short.
Ex	Maybe we should all go to a keep-fit class.
Dee	Oh? Who's going to pay, Mr Wallet?
Ex	Me.
Aitch	What? Did I hear Ex offering other people his money?
Jay	We need this down in writing.
Em	I used to go swimming a lot. But –

Bee	But?
Em	They had a great chocolate machine there and a chip shop next door, which kind of put back on what I'd just exercised off.
Dee	Life's cruel.
Ex	There's always line-dancing.
Jay	Yee-hah!
Ex	I've taken it up. It's really good. Tones up your thighs.
Dee	And I'll bet you look real purty in your cowboy-boots, Tex.
Ex	I sure do, Miss Dee.
Aitch	The music's terrible!
Ex	You don't know what you're talking about.
Aitch	It's all swing-your-partner music and dos-ee-dos, isn't it?
Ex	That's SQUARE-dancing, Dope.
Aitch	Oh. It's all rubbish, anyway.
Ex	What is?
Aitch	It's just posing to music in tight jeans. You want locking up.
Ex	Do you want a fight?
Aitch	Not with you, Lone Ranger, no.
Em	Oh, please. Fisticuffs.
Dee	Male brute-strength. Or is that, brute male-strength?
Bee	It could be 'stupid show-off blokes' you're looking for.
Dee	THAT'S the one.
Ex	Just for that, we won't let you watch.
Bee	Oh, please!
Dee	We'll be ever so quiet.
Jay	I won't. I'll be shouting 'Go on! Smash his face in!'
Bee	To whom?
Jay	To both of them. Fair's fair.
Bee	You're so cute.
Jay	I know. It's keeping away from the chips that does it.

The bell rings.

Dee Registration.

Jay What? Already? But I haven't finished everybody's chips yet.

Ex This is ridiculous. They should supply us with doggy-bags.

Em Come on. Let's go. What you got this afternoon, Jay?

Jay Shakespeare assignment with Year 8.

Em I'm doing poetry. Mr Owen and Mr Brooke.

Ex I've got football. Got to get there before Year 10 decide to dive into the gym to climb up the wall-bars like gorillas. See ya.

Ex runs off.

Jay Can I get a lift home after school, Dee?

Dee Yeah, if you can wait till quarter-past four. I've got Tracey Fenton in detention.

Jay Oh! Poor Frankie! He'll be pining for her!

Dee Shame.

Jay See you later, then.

Jay walks off with Em.

Aitch Anyone seen my teacher's planner?

Bee You're sitting on it.

Aitch Oh. Come on. I'll walk you to your form.

Bee Why?

Aitch Because I know you've got some biscuits there that I can take back to MY room.

Bee You're so thoughtful. – YOU, LAD! What do you think you're doing?! Get to registration! – Tut! Kids are SO immature.

Aitch Not like us.

Bee Quite.

FRIENDS

Cast: *Rav*
Josh
Carrie
Tom
Leanne
Teacher (male)

Scene: *The classroom. The pupils are waiting for the teacher to arrive. Carrie, Rav, Josh and Leanne are all sitting together. Tom is sitting alone across the other side of the room.*

Rav	Has anyone seen two pounds?
Josh	Two pounds of what?
Rav	I've lost two pound coins. It's my dinner-money, too.
Carrie	Did you drop them on the floor?
Rav	No. I've looked.
Carrie	Did you have them with you last lesson?
Rav	I don't know. I had them at breaktime when we were standing by the machines.
Carrie	Oh. That's terrible.
Josh	Is this a trick to make me pay for the pictures after school this afternoon? Because it won't work.
Carrie	Oh, just help look, will you?
Josh	I'm looking. I'm looking.
Tom	(*coming over*) Have you dropped this quid? I saw it in the doorway and I've just heard what you said.
Rav	Thanks, Tom! Excellent!
Tom	No problem.
	Tom goes back to his seat.
Carrie	What's the matter with him?
Josh	Who?

Carrie	Tom. He never sits with anyone.
Rav	I know. At breaktime he's always on his own, leaning up against the wall. Why doesn't he join in with someone? It's good of him to hand the money over, though. Some wouldn't.
Leanne	I think he's grubby-looking and weird. I think he looks funny.
Josh	And YOU do with that chocolate stuck in your gob. Give me some.
Leanne	No. Buy your own.
Josh	I gave you some of mine yesterday.
Leanne	So? I never asked you for it. – There's something wrong with that Tom kid.
Josh	There's something wrong with you as well, Leanne.
Leanne	Oh yeah? Well, go and ask him over to our group, then. Go on. If you like him so much, he can be your best friend and you can drag him around after you. He can go round your house as well!
Josh	I didn't say anything about friends.
Carrie	It's just a shame he's on his own all the time.
Leanne	Well, go and sit by him then. Who's stopping you?
Rav	Shut up. Teacher's here.
Teacher	Good morning, everyone. Sit down, please. Right, now I thought that this lesson we'd have a discussion about friendship. Based on? Yes, Rav?
Rav	The book we're reading, Sir.
Teacher	That's right. Because the book we're reading is all about that group of friends at school and how they get on with each other, isn't it? So, I'd like you to get into groups of five . . .
Leanne	Oh, no! That means we'll get Tom in our group, I bet.
Teacher	Yes, Leanne?
Leanne	Nothing, Sir.
Teacher	Don't talk when I'm speaking, thank you. – Right, Class, I'm going to write a few points on the board for you to discuss in your groups, and then we'll

	listen to what each group has to say. Get into groups, then.
Leanne	Here it comes.
Teacher	Tom? Would you like to work with Rav's group?
Leanne	Told you.
Tom	Could I just do some writing instead, Sir?
Teacher	No. I want you to join in with everyone else. It's good to get involved with the rest of the class. – Rav, Tom will be in your group.
Rav	Yes, Sir. – Sit yourself down, Tom. – Right. First point off the board is . . . 'What makes a good friend?' Who's going to start, then?
Leanne	Has he GOT to be in our group?
Tom	I didn't want to come over here. Sir made me.
Leanne	Please!
Carrie	Oh, shut up, Leanne.
Tom	I'll move if you want.
Carrie	You're all right there, Tom.
Josh	I'll start.
Carrie	Go on, then, Josh. Say something brilliant like you usually do.
Josh	What I look for in a friend is chocolate.
Carrie	I knew it. A brilliant answer from Josh. Thank you, Josh.
Rav	Chocolate? What are you on about?
Josh	I would be friends with anyone who had some chocolate and who gave me some of it. So Leanne wouldn't score very highly.
Leanne	Who's bothered?
Rav	A very deep answer from Josh there.
Josh	Not in the least. I am a very shallow person and I admit it. Have Twix, will travel.
Rav	Can someone say something serious, please? Sir's going to be asking us for our answers in a minute.

Josh	All right, all right. Er – having something in common. Friends should have something in common.
Rav	A fine opinion. Well worth waiting for.
Josh	No applause please.
Carrie	I look for honesty in a friend.
Rav	Good point. Honesty.
Carrie	Because if someone's honest with you, you know they mean what they say and you can trust them. Like, if I had to leave my coat for a minute with a friend, I know I could trust them to look after it for me.
Rav	Because they're honest and will stay with the coat like they promised and not walk off and leave it?
Carrie	Yeah. Something like that.
Rav	So – you'd leave your coat with Josh, then? He IS your friend, you know.
Carrie	Josh would sell it for a KitKat. What about you, Rav?
Rav	I think a friend should be kind. I mean, that's just a basic. They should be very caring and supportive. What do YOU think, Tom?
Tom	Well, I –
Leanne	Wait a minute! What about me?
Rav	I asked Tom.
Leanne	Oh, thanks very much. Some friend YOU are!
Rav	Take no notice, Tom. What do YOU look for in a friend?
Tom	I don't know. I haven't got any friends.
Leanne	See? What's the point in asking HIM?
Carrie	What? No friends at all, Tom?
Tom	No.
Carrie	Why not?
Leanne	Because he's grubby and he smells. That's why not.
Josh	Stay out of it, Leanne!
Leanne	You gonna make me, Josh?
Teacher	What's going on over there?

Rav	Nothing, Sir. It's all right.
Josh	Just discussing a point, Sir.
Teacher	I hope so.
Josh	(*quietly*) The one sticking out the top of Leanne's head.
Leanne	You think you're SO funny, don't you, Josh?
Josh	I do actually, yeah.
Carrie	Let's get back to what we were talking about. – Why haven't you got any friends, Tom?
Tom	I don't know. People just don't seem to bother with me. I suppose it's because of my clothes and that.
Carrie	Oh, no. Leanne was just being stupid when she said that.
Leanne	I wasn't.
Tom	But my dad hasn't worked for ages and there's only the two of us since Mum left . . . There just isn't the money for any new uniform clothes yet.
Carrie	Same here. My mum hasn't worked for ages either and there's just the two of US. But at least we've got my nan to help us out a bit. I know how you feel.
Rav	I'm sure if you'd just talk to people you'd make friends.
Josh	Yeah. You're doing all right with us, aren't you?
Tom	I suppose so.
Leanne	(*sarcastically*) This is REALLY touching.
Rav	Okay, Leanne. Your turn. What do you want to add to the discussion?
Leanne	To this discussion? Nothing!
Carrie	You're just being really difficult today. What's the matter with you?
Leanne	Ask me what I look for in a friend!
Rav	I just DID and you had a wobbler!
Leanne	Ask me what I look for in a FRIEND!
Josh	Leanne! What do you look for in a friend?

Leanne	LOYALTY! Sticking by your friends and not skanking them the second someone new comes into the group!
Josh	Oo! Temper, temper! Just because you're not coming out too well in this discussion.
Leanne	What do you mean by that?
Josh	We've all decided that a friend should be kind.
Carrie	And you're not.
Josh	And supportive.
Rav	And you're not.
Josh	And that friends should have something in common.
Carrie	And I, for one, don't know what I've got in common with you any more, Leanne.
Leanne	You stuck-up snobs, the lot of you. I'm not sitting here any longer. I'm going over the other side of the room to sit on my own. Where's my bag? Oh!!
Tom	You've upturned it all on the floor. I'll help you put it all back in your bag.
Leanne	I'll do it myself, thank you. – I said, I can do it myself!
Rav	What's all this chocolate doing in here?
Josh	There's stacks. And you wouldn't give ME any!
Leanne	It's mine. I got it from the machine.
Carrie	You said you didn't have any money with you today. Where'd you get the money from?
Leanne	You calling me a thief?!
Teacher	What's going on here? What are you people doing on the floor?
Tom	Leanne's bag upturned on the floor, Sir. We were just helping to put it all back in. It's all right now, Sir.
Carrie	No need to cover, Tom. It's not all right at all. – Answer my question, Leanne. Where'd you get the money from?
Rav	Wait a sec. I've got a hole in my pocket. That's how my money fell out. By the machine, was it, Leanne?

	I checked my money at the machine, put it in my pocket – and then suddenly you've got a bag full of chocolate!
Leanne	Well, aren't we the great detective, Rav?!
Rav	I might be! Why?!
Leanne	'Cause you've got your story wrong, Sherlock! I borrowed the money off Tracey Kemp! And it's nothing to do with you anyway! But why don't you ask her? You obviously don't trust ME any more! Not now you've got your new friend, Tom!
Teacher	That is quite enough! Where do you two think you are?! I will not have shouting in my classroom! Now – the two of you! Outside with me and sort this out.

Teacher takes Rav and Leanne outside.

Josh	Honesty.
Carrie	What?
Josh	That was the final point she failed. Honesty.
Carrie	No, she didn't. I just asked Tracey. She DID lend Leanne the money.
Josh	Really?
Carrie	Really.
Josh	Oh. – Still, that's not the point now though, is it? The point is, does anyone want a friend with a vicious attitude like Leanne's? Honest or not.
Carrie	Does anyone want a friend who doesn't trust them and accuses them wrongly? It works both ways, Josh.
Josh	I'm not like Leanne. Nowhere near it. – Why, Carrie – are you?
Carrie	Why do you ask? Don't you know me? You should do. We're friends. Aren't we?
Josh	I'm not getting into all this. Are we still all going to the pictures after school?
Carrie	Might as well. I don't suppose Leanne'll be coming now. D'you want to come, Tom?
Tom	Me?

Carrie No. The bloke behind you. Yes, you. Well?

Tom Yeah. Great. I'll see if Dad'll let me have some money.

Josh I'll pay. You can give me the money back tomorrow. I trust you.

Carrie Yeah. You've got an honest face, Tom.

Josh Trust AND honesty. Well, well. Sounds like the start of a beautiful friendship.

Carrie Oh dear, Tom. I'd run for it now while you've still got the chance!

CARING

Cast: *Jay, a male student*
Teacher, a woman
Uncle Jack (Jack)
Tina, Jay's friend

Scene: *Jay wandering through the day.*

Jay speaks to the audience.

Jay People keep telling me how lucky I am to have such caring people around me. But, to tell you the truth, I'm a bit tired of hearing it.

Teacher Do you know WHY I want your homework in on time, Jay?

Jay My teacher. One of them anyway. They all blur into one sometimes. 'Cause sometimes they all say the same thing. They CARE.

Teacher Because I CARE.

Jay There. Told you.

Teacher Because I care about your standard of work and the grades you could get. The future you could have if only YOU cared. Don't you care, Jay?

Jay answers the teacher.

Jay Not really. No.

Teacher Then you should! – There. You've made me lose my temper again. Let's see if I can keep calm, shall I?

Jay If you want. I just don't see the point, Miss.

Teacher Well I DO. What is wrong? Why have you become like this? You used to be so full of life – and now . . .

Jay Now I'm a dead-loss? A waste of space? Is that what the teachers are saying? I'll bet it is. All of them. They don't care.

Teacher They DO care. YOU'RE the one that doesn't care, Jay. Come to homework club if there's a problem with working at home. IS there a problem with working at home? Or is there just a problem? Something you could tell me. You can tell me anything, Jay. Anything at all. I won't be shocked. – Something to do with that fight you were in yesterday? You were lucky not to get suspended, you know that?

Jay Yeah. I know.

Teacher Do you know why you weren't? Because people cared enough to sort it out another way. You're lucky it was just a bit of shoving you and Darren were up to. A punch would have meant you down the road.

Jay I know.

Teacher So. What's the problem?

Jay turns to the audience.

Jay I couldn't tell her. I can't tell her. I'm not ready. But I can't work at home. Or anywhere.

Jack Coming to play football, Jay? A good game of kickabout will soon blow the clouds away.

Jay My Uncle Jack. He thinks football solves everything. I used to think the same.

Jack Well?

Jay speaks to Uncle Jack.

Jay I can't. I'm doing my homework.

Jack I wish you were. But it was a good try. You nearly had me convinced there for a second. – I – er – heard from your dad today.

Jay Not interested.

Jack He's very well. Sends his love.

Jay I'll bet he does. And his new wife? Does she send her love, too?

Jack She's – er – pregnant.

Jay speaks to the audience.

Jay The shock cut through me. Straight to the brain. I put on my usual not-bothered face for Uncle Jack,

	though. (*to Uncle Jack*) That puts me well and truly out of the picture then, doesn't it?
Jack	Your dad still loves you, Jay.
Jay	If he loved me, why did he leave? He's YOUR brother. You tell me.
Jack	He was always a bit useless, your dad. Never could stick to anything. We'd be having a game of footie, he'd get bored and wander off. He'd go out with Carol one week and Wendy the next. It wasn't that he didn't care – he was just – immature. Couldn't deal with responsibility. Certainly couldn't deal with your mother.
Jay	Serves him right that she ran out on him. How did HE like it? And how do YOU like raising your brother's child, Uncle Jack? Don't I stop you from having a family of your own? Don't I put the women off knowing that they might be saddled with me if they settle down with you? Don't you hate me?
Jack	No. I love you. I care about you, Jay. And I'll never leave you. Even though you are a right little moaner.
	Jay speaks to the audience again.
Jay	And then he threw me on the floor and sat on me until I said I loved him, too. His usual way of winning an argument. I DO like being with him. I used to like kicking a ball about and being fouled by him all the time. He has to cheat, you see, 'cause he's getting on a bit now. He's thirty. And I know he cares, I KNOW . . . But I just can't be like I used to be . . . It's really difficult.
Tina	You're being really difficult again, Jay.
Jay	Tina. My best friend. We do our homework together and talk about everything. Mostly about me these days. She talked me through the early days of Mum and Dad leaving. She's always been there for me. (*to Tina*) How am I being difficult?
Tina	Are you going to help with this Science project or what?
Jay	I'm not much interested in a stupid Science project.

Tina	Well I am! This is important to me. And it should be important to you.
Jay	It isn't. I've got other things to worry about.
Tina	You're just not trying. You're not trying with this Science project and you're not trying to deal with your life the way it is.
Jay	I don't like my life the way it is.
	Pause.
Tina	Look, I can't make your mum and dad come back!
Jay	Okay, okay. No need to shout. Why is everybody shouting at me?
Tina	No one's shouting at you!
Jay	There! See? You're shouting again!
Tina	They're frustrated with you. They don't know what to do to make you happy.
Jay	Who wants them to make me happy?
Tina	You don't know how lucky you are.
Jay	Oh, not again!
Tina	You're clever, you do well at school and you've got your Uncle Jack to look after you. There are some kids in our school who would kill to be in the position you're in. Look at poor Matty! Brother got knocked down by a car. Matty's really struggling to get over it – but he IS trying and we're all helping. We all had a party at Karen's house that you wouldn't come to.
Jay	I did.
Tina	For five minutes. Then you made your usual speech about life not being fair, how nobody understood and then you left. Having nearly upset Matty and everyone else.
Jay	You're supposed to be my friend. You're supposed to stick by me! Whatever I do!
Tina	No. No, I'm not. I won't stick by someone miserable who gets into fights and is starting to get into trouble with his teachers.

Jay	Do you know why I had a fight with Darren?
Tina	No. Why don't you tell me? Let's talk about YOU some more!
Jay	He said my mum ran off with the man next door.
Tina	But she did!
Jay	My life's ruined and nobody understands but me.
Tina	There's no point talking to you when you're like this. Self-destructive. If you don't care about yourself, neither do I. I'm going home to do this Science project on my own. 'Phone me when you've grown up.

Jay speaks to the audience.

Jay	Tina's right of course. I am destroying myself. And I'm destroying my friendship with her. She can't make my mum and dad come back. No one can. Life goes on. Dad has got a new family starting. And Mum . . . I don't even know where she is . . . And me? I'm stuck. With myself.
Teacher	So? Where do we go from here? Get into more fights? Get suspended? Fail all your exams? Blow your chances of college?
Jack	Spend your life waiting for your mum and dad to come back? Not join in the football? Not join in the fun?
Tina	Make no more friends? Switch me right off?
Teacher	That's silly.
Jack	That's sad.
Tina	That's selfish. Don't you care? About yourself? Be honest. No more blocking me out with glib remarks just because you're unhappy.
Jay	All right. – I care.
Tina	Then make a decision. Be responsible. DO something.

Jay speaks to the audience.

Jay	Life goes on. That's the bottom line. And so do I. – But it's tough. Am I going to lose Tina and Uncle

Jack? Am I going to louse up my exams – even if it does seem like pointless paper-chasing at the moment? Let's face it – I'm stupid. But I'm not THAT stupid. – It's just . . . the ache gets really bad some days. And I hear that only time will heal it. – People keep telling me how lucky I am to have such caring people around me. They're right. But, to tell you the truth, I'm just tired of hearing it.

FRUSTRATION

Cast: *Tank, a teenage boy*
Gismo, a teenage boy
Gracie, a teenage girl
Cat, a teenage girl

Scene: *Four friends meeting to play 'Frustration', the famous pop-a-matic board game. They come prepared to make an evening of it – big bags of crisps, big bottles of pop – each one entering almost ceremoniously with something to eat or drink. It is their Friday-night ritual. The game is covered with a cloth until it is time to play.*

Tank (*entering with massive bag of crisps*) 'Evening, everybody. Let the games commence.
He puts the crisps down and takes his seat at the table.

Gismo Not those crisps again! No one liked them last time.

Tank Gracie did.

Gismo She doesn't fancy you, I keep telling ya.

Tank Not yet. But she will.

Gismo Oh, yeah?

Tank Yeah. She'll succumb to me Ready Salted.

Gismo I don't think so, Sad-Boy.
He dumps down a bottle of pop and sits down.

Tank Where's Cat? She's usually here by now.

Gismo She'll be along any minute, no doubt. Her and her dated vocabulary.

Tank Dated vocabulary? I like the way she speaks. It's very groovy.

Gismo Groovy! Listen to yourself. You're as bad as her. She's a 'sixties-freak. With her fake-leather zip-up tops and psychedelic skirts.

Tank (*imagining her*) I like her fake-leather zip-up tops and psychedelic skirts.

Gismo She buys old *Avengers* videos and collects James Bond memorabilia!

Tank (*still imagining her*) I like her fake-leather zip-up tops and –

Gismo Oh, behave! You're girl-mad, you are.

Tank I love it when she says 'Miaow, Comrades'. She's so groovy AND politically aware.

Gismo Sad-Boy.

Cat (*entering, waves groovily*) Miaow, Comrades.

Tank Oo! She said it!

Gismo Get a grip.

Tank (*giving the peace-sign*) Deep groove, Feline-Fave.

Gismo How goes it, Cat?

Cat A day of bad vibes, Gismo-Babe. IT, double Science, chip-famine at dinnertime, forgot my English book –

Gismo }
Tank } (*aware of how bad this is*) Ooo!

Gismo Detention?

Cat No. Lecture on stupidity.

Tank Bad luck. Have a crisp.

Cat Urgh! Not those!

Gismo She's only got nine lives, Tank. They'd use up at least five.

Tank They're for Gracie.

Cat They won't work, Tank.

Gismo He should be more like James Bond, shouldn't he, Cat? Shaken, but not stirred. Licensed to kill.

Cat He'll kill her with those crisps.

Tank What YOU got, then, oh exotic one?

Cat (*producing a huge box*) Jaffa Cakes.

She sits down.

Tank	A woman of taste. As anyone can see from that top.
Gismo	Oh, behave!
Tank	(*sees Gracie enter*) She's here! Stand by your beds!
Gracie	Sorry I'm late.

She sticks small box on table and plonks herself down.

Gismo	Hey! What about a bit of respect and ceremony for the great Friday-night ritual that is –
Tank **Gismo** **Cat**	(*meeting index-fingers like the Musketeers, or some other bonding-sign*) 'Frustration'.
Gismo	The exciting –
Cat **Tank**	Pop-a-matic –
Gismo	Board game.
Gracie	On your bike, Gismo. I've just had to cook the tea and bath my baby brother before I came out tonight.
Cat	(*pointing to box*) What are those?
Gracie	After Eights.
Tank	She's so sophisticated. No one else would have thought of them, Gracie. You're so brilliant in the way that you could have brought anything to the feast – Jammie Dodgers, bumper bag of Twix – but you had more style than that. You –
Cat	(*tweaking Tank's temple-hair*) Terminate the conversation, Tank. You've gone into overload.
Tank	Ow! Soz.

He rubs his temple after Cat has released it.

Gismo	'Terminate the conversation, Tank'? That's very modern of you, Cat. Don't you mean 'Hold the 'phone, Baby'?
Cat	Got a problem with the way I talk, Gismo?
Gismo	No. I love listening to you speak. It's like being part of a real cool scene, man.
Cat	I'll ignore your hostile vibes. Shall we begin?

All	(*as Cat takes the cloth that covers the game, pressing the bubble underneath to make it click*) Click! (*as she removes the cloth with a dramatic sweep, releasing the bubble to pop*) Pop!! *All applaud.*
Tank	Game on! Bags me Yellow.
Gismo	Like the streak running down your back. And I'll be Red.
Tank	Like the colour of your eyes, Vampire-Boy.
Gismo	Shut it.
Cat	Which do you want, Gracie?
Gracie	Green?
Cat	Sure.
Tank	See? What a good choice! Green is such a sensitive colour. It's – *They silence him with a look.*
Tank	Soz.
Cat	And I'll be Cool Blue.
Gismo	I'll go first. *He reaches for the bubble.*
Gracie	(*smacking his hand away*) Arrogance puts you last. Tank, you can go first.
Gismo	I protest!
Tank	(*totally knocked out by this*) I'm – You are so – (*gets out a filthy hankie*) I'm sorry, I'm filling up. *He gives a BIG blow of his nose.*
Cat **Gismo**⎬ Urgh! **Gracie**	
Cat	Gross-a-mundo!
Tank	I'm just so moved.
Gismo	You're getting Cat mad, Tank. She's going to karate-chop you in a minute.
Cat	I'm ignoring this . . .
Gismo	Or maybe strap you to a table and laser-cut you in half, Mr Bond.

Cat	Just hit the bubble, Tank!
Tank	(*pops*) Two.
Cat	(*pops*) Four.
Gismo	(*pops*) Three.
Gracie	(*pops*) Six!

She puts her piece on the track.

Tank	She's out!
Gracie	(*pops*) Six! (*moves piece six and pops*) Six!!

She gets another piece out.

Gismo	She must be cheating!
Tank	(*standing to beat him up*) Step outside!
Cat	(*pulling him onto his chair*) Cool it, Tank!
Gracie	(*pops*) Six!

She moves another six.

Gismo	She must be tilting the table!
Gracie	(*pops*) Four. (*moves*)
Gismo	Thank goodness for that!
Tank	(*pops*) Two.
Cat	(*pops*) Four.
Gismo	This'll be it this time. A six. (*pops*) One.
Tank	(*to Gismo*) Loser.
Gracie	(*pops*) Six!

She moves a piece out.

Gismo	I don't believe it!
Cat	Patience is a right-on virtue, Gismo-Babe.
Gismo	Been reading joss-stick packets again, Kitty-Kat?
Cat	Oh! Hostility zone minus three!
Gracie	(*pops*) Six!
Tank	Again?
Gracie	(*pops*) Six! (*moves pieces, pops*) Six! (*moves pieces*) One home.
Cat	There's something unnatural at work here.
Gismo	Oh! Hostility zone minus twenty, Emma Peel!

Gracie	(*pops*) Six! (*the table suddenly moves*) Who did that?
Gismo	Four!
Gracie	It was a six! Somebody shoved the table!
Gismo	Nobody shoved the table! (*pops*) Two! Sad! I'm sick of this!
Tank	It's MY turn, DipStick! (*pops*) Two! Sad! I'm sick of this!
Cat	No patience.
Gismo	(*pops*) Two! Sad!
Cat	It's my stinking turn, Flat-Head!!
Gismo	It isn't!!
Cat	It is! It's Tank, me, THEN you, then her.
Gracie	Her? Oh, that's nice, isn't it?! I wish I hadn't bothered coming! And stop playing footsie with me under the table, Tank!
Tank	I never!
Gracie **Gismo** **Cat**	} You did!
Gismo	You were playing it with ME a minute ago!
Tank	I thought she had big feet all of a sudden.
Cat	(*pops*) One! Purple pain!
Gismo	Yah! (*pops*) Two! Again? There's something wrong with this board! I'm gonna give it a shake!
Cat	Shake that board and I'll shake your nose, Comrade!
Gismo	Do your worst, Stalin!
Cat	Don't!
	Gismo stands and grabs the board but they all lunge at him and sit him down again, holding onto him in their fury. They are all frozen onto him now, breathing heavily.
Cat	Okay. Let's just cool it, People. Ease down into a cosmically serene state and breathe in.
	They all breathe in.
Cat	And out.

They all breathe out.

Cat Now. This is just a game. And we are going to be really mellow about this and we are going to let go of Gismo.

Tank He'll wreck the board the minute we let go of him!

Cat No, he won't. Will you, Gizzy-Baby?

Gismo won't speak.

Tank See?! Just because he's jealous of Gracie winning!

Gracie (*touched by this*) Thanks, Tank.

Tank I'm just telling it like it is.

Gismo Oh! Lawman!

Cat We're going to let go now, Gismo. And I know you won't let me down, because if you do, I'm gonna suck your brains out. Is it cool, Baby?

Gismo It's cool.

Cat Okay. After three. One. Two. Three.

They all let go. Gismo stands up and shakes the board everywhere like a mad Flamenco dancer, pieces flying all over the place!

Gismo Ariba! Ariba! Yee-ha!

Cat Gismo! You're dead!!

Cat chases Gismo round the table, Tank and Gracie cheering her on.

Gismo Same time next week, Comrades?!

He grabs the After Eights and exits running.

Cat Gismo!!!

She exits, running after him.

Gracie He took my After Eights!

Tank (*puts an arm round her*) There, there. (*offers bag with the other hand*) Ready Salted?

Gracie Oh, not those again! Get lost! (*exits*)

Tank (*to audience*) Not yet. But she will. Next week.

GENTS

Cast: *Fred*
       Jack
       Trev

Scene: *A park bench. Fred, Jack and Trev – all in their seventies – are having a chat. Trev, however, has fallen asleep in the middle of it.*

Fred So I said to him, I said, 'Don't you ride your bike that close to my car, you young tear-away! I'll tan your backside for you!' I said.

Jack You know their trouble? They've no respect for other people's property. Now, then.

Fred I'll tell you their trouble. They've got no respect for other people's property.

Jack I just said that. – Fred. Fred!

Fred What?

Jack You've turned your hearing-aid off again!

Fred Eh?

Jack I said, you've turned your hearing-aid off again!!

Fred (*looking about him*) Lemonade? I haven't got any lemonade. I'll ask Trev. Oy! Trev!

Trev (*waking up*) Stand by your beds!! – What? Oh. It's you, Fred.

Fred Jack wants some lemonade.

Jack (*tiredly*) No, I don't.

Trev Lemonade? What do I look like? A bloody corner-shop?

Jack I said HEARING-AID!! Oh, you tell him, Trev! He's turned the stupid thing off again.

Trev (*to Fred, pointing to his ear*) Oy! Your hearing-aid's off again, you daft old duffer!

Fred	Is it? Oh.
	He switches it back on. The hearing-aid gives a huge whistle as Fred tries to settle it.
Jack	Oh, bleeding hell!
Trev	Sort the cowing thing out, Fred!
Fred	Poor old thing. It needs a bit of an MOT.
Jack	Who doesn't?
Trev	(*spotting a woman walking towards them*) Hey! Look! It's Norman Beresford's widow!
Jack	Oh, she's a fine-looking woman is Norman Beresford's widow.
Fred	Big, sturdy legs. I like a woman with big, sturdy legs.
Trev	Shut up. She'll hear you.
	Their eyes follow the imaginary Evelyn Beresford as she walks past them.
Trev	'Morning, Evelyn.
Jack	Lovely day.
Fred	You've got big, sturdy –
	Trev and Jack jump on Fred.
Trev	Shut up, you great nit!
Jack	No. Sorry, Evelyn. He didn't say anything. He sneezed. (*whispering to Fred*) Sneeze, idiot.
Fred	A – choo!
Jack	See?
Trev	Yes! See you at the social tonight. Ta-rar a bit, Evelyn.
Fred	She's gone. You can let go of me now.
	Jack and Trev let go of Fred.
Trev	Fool! You nearly ruined me chances for a Ladies' Excuse-Me there!
Jack	You reckon she'll ask you tonight?
Trev	Certainly. I'm still a fine figure of a man. Still got all me own teeth, you know.
Jack	I've got somebody else's.
Fred	(*fiddling with his hearing-aid*) You've broken this, grabbing me like you did. I'll have to fix it now.

There is another terrible, eardrum-shattering whistle from the hearing-aid.

Jack Dear me, Fred!

Trev That stinking contraption!

Silence.

Jack Thank goodness for that!

Trev You want to get that seen to. I don't know how your Edie puts up with you.

Fred She just whips the batteries out.

A momentary pause. Trev gets some sweets out.

Jack Giz us one, Trev.

Trev Get your own.

Jack Just one.

Trev Go on, then.

Jack What are they?

Trev Treacle toffees.

Jack Oh, no! That's ruddy deliberate, that is!

Trev What is?

Jack You always get toffees because you know I can't eat them.

Fred Why not?

Jack They get stuck to me plate.

Fred I'll have one.

He takes a sweet and sticks it in his mouth.

Jack What about YOUR plate? You've got dentures, too.

Fred It don't bother me. I just get it into a nice, slick wedge onto me top-plate and let it melt.

He takes out his top-plate to show them.

See?

Trev Your teeth are filthy, Fred.

Jack Why ain't you cleaned them?

Fred Run out of Domestos.

Trev Domestos?!

Jack You're supposed to use Steradent, you great clod!

Fred	Ah, but you get a lovely finish with Domestos. Lovely gleam.
Trev	You're gonna bloody poison yourself, you are.
Fred	Nah! I give them a good rinse under the tap and polish them up on the tea-towel. When Edie's not looking, of course.
Jack	You're terrible to that woman of yours, you are, Fred.
Trev	You don't appreciate her.
Jack	I wish our Rose was still alive.
Trev	She was a good wench was your Rose, Jack.
Jack	She was. Did everything for me. Kept the house clean. Cooked me dinner. Oh, she did a lovely stew did our Rose.
Trev	That's true. Maggie was good at puddings.
Jack	She was. Very true.
Trev	I'd have walked across broken glass for her Spotted Dick.
Jack	And her rhubarb and custard never had you galloping to the bog after, did it?
Trev	No. She was one in a million was our Maggie.
Fred	Edie wouldn't give me no pudding the other night.
Trev	Well, I wouldn't either if you polished your teeth on me tea-towel!
Fred	Jam Roly-Poly. Looked nice as well.
	Silence.
Fred	Are we off to the betting shop now, are we?
Jack	Gee-gees or dogs?
Fred	Dogs. I've been given a tip.
Trev	From who?
Fred	It's a dead-cert.
Jack	From WHO?
Fred	Arthur.
Jack	Arthur?! Don't make me laugh! What does he know about dogs?
Trev	Dead-cert? Dead-loss, more like!

Fred No. It's a good bet. Rollicking Ronnie in the 2.30.

Jack Rubbish. Last time Arthur gave you a bet, the dog had piles!

Trev Yeah! It wouldn't even come out of the starting-box. Just sat there, scratching itself.

Fred Well, I'm putting a fiver on it anyway.

Jack You'll do no such thing.

Trev We won't let you.

Jack You've got something else to spend your money on.

Trev and Jack get up and help Fred up.

Trev Come on. Let's get moving.

Fred Where we going?

Jack The town.

Fred Why?

Trev To get your missus some new tea-towels!

GENDER

Cast: *Baz*
Brian
Brendan
Sue
Sasha
Sarah

Scene: *The boys stand together in a line, giving their opinions in a formal presentation to an audience. The girls are doing the same. A television and video are nearby for use in the presentation, plus mounts for diagram-charts.*

Baz Today my colleagues and I will be discussing the issue of gender. Isn't that right, Brian?

Brian Yes. Thanks, Baz. That's right. I will just explain the term 'gender' for the girls in the room. It means what sex you are – a boy or a girl.

Baz Thanks for clearing that up for us, Brian.

Brian No problem. These terms are a little difficult for girls to understand.

Baz I'd like to ask Brendan to start us off on the differences between boys and girls. All those little things that make us so – well, different. Over to you, Brendan.

Brendan Thanks, Baz. Well, the differences between boys and girls are obvious from the beginning. As babies, boys are bigger and stronger and pick up things very quickly, whereas girls just tend to lie there for the first few months dribbling and looking like what they are. The weaker sex.

Baz Which is the term we still use for girls, isn't it, Brendan? The weaker sex?

Brendan That's right, Baz. And this idea of being the weaker sex is soon taken on by the girls. In nursery school,

	or just within the home, girls are quite happy playing with dolls and making imaginary tea in plastic tea-services. On the other hand, boys are running around, building with Lego, playing sports and generally doing more important and constructive things. Isn't that right, Brian?
Brian	It certainly is, Brendan. At school, girls are more interested in learning to cook and sew, paint a picture, make a blouse – that is, learn things which are going to be of use to them in their adult lives.
Baz	You mean, when they become wives and mothers?
Brian	That's right.
Baz	Because that's all girls are really interested in, looking after men and children?
Brian	That's just about it. I mean, of course they'll need a bit of English so that they can read a book to their children and learn a bit of Maths for when it comes to doing the shopping – but, as I say, they don't need to know anything more than that.
Baz	Just wanted to clear that point up, Brian.
Brian	No problem.
Brendan	If we could just take a look at this diagram of a girl which will make the point even clearer.
Baz	Fine. Over to you, Brendan.
Brendan	Look – small hands just right for picking up small babies or a needle to sew with. A small frame generally which makes them biologically more suited to being in small work-areas like the kitchen and the bathroom and making them suitable for getting into small places within the home for cleaning purposes.
Baz	Weak muscles, too, so much better that the boy should be the one trained for the work-place and that the girl should be allowed to protect those weak muscles by stopping at home and doing a bit of washing-up.
Brendan	That's right, Baz. Good point.

Brian	And the big eyes would be for . . .?
Brendan	Well, obviously, for looking sadly at the male when she has done something wrong so that he will forgive her, thereby not causing the relationship to break up.
Brian	I see. Well, some really interesting points there for us to bear in mind from a biological point of view.
Baz	And then there's the difference in academic success or –
Brian	For any girls in the audience –
Baz	How boys and girls get on differently at school with their exams.
Brian	Boys, obviously, are more clever, having been able to concentrate more on their studying instead of having to worry about other things.
Brendan	Like the things girls worry about all the time.
Baz	Like their hair.
Brendan	Make-up.
Baz	Clothes.
Brian	Nails.
Brendan	Bosoms.
Baz	Spots and –
Brian	Boys.
Brendan	With all these worries, they just don't have time to study as well.
Baz	Which is why the boys get all the good jobs when they leave school like –
Brian	Managers.
Brendan	Doctors.
Baz	Professors.
Brian	Engineers.
Brendan	Solicitors.
Baz	Oil tycoons, etc.
Brian	Whereas girls just become –
Brendan	Check-out girls and –

Baz	Hairdressers.
Brian	That is unless they become wives and mothers, allowing their men to look after them.
Brendan	It can, therefore, be concluded that who you are and what you do depends on your gender.
Baz	Because life is different for boys and girls. Thank you. Any questions? No? Then I'd like to hand over to the girls for 'their side of the story', as it were, to use a feminine phrase. Over to you, Ladies.
Sue	Thank you. Well, Sasha, Sarah and myself have a totally different view of the issue of gender, I must say, to our male colleagues.
Sasha	That's right, Sue. A totally different view. Over to you, Sarah.
Sarah	Thanks, Sasha. Well, the difference, as we see it, between boys and girls is two-fold.
Sue	Er – sorry to stop you, Sarah. Could you just explain the term 'two-fold' for any boys in the audience? It IS rather complicated for them.
Sarah	No problem. A 'two-fold' difference is one which has two parts to it. Two coming after one, of course, numerically. Sorry – number-wise.
Sue	Thanks for clearing that up, Sarah.
Sarah	Sure. The two-fold difference is that one, girls make more effort than boys, and two, girls are more AWARE.
Sasha	That's aware in the sense of what, Sarah?
Sarah	In the sense of being AWAKE mostly, or, at least, in the sense of having some SENSE.
Sasha	An interesting point. If I could just explore that a little, Sarah.
Sarah	Of course, Sasha.
Sasha	It is a sad fact of life that girls are born with more sense and therefore they put more effort into what they do. As babies, girls sit up and take notice of the world around them – noticing the shapes, colours and textures of their environment. Boys merely have

an urge to stick a bottle of milk in their mouths and scream for attention – and more milk, of course. The greatest instinct for a girl is to learn. The only instinct for a boy is to eat. Sue?

Sue Thanks, Sasha. If we look at this diagram of a boy, this point can be emphasised. Look – huge hands, just right for grabbing as much food as possible. Beady eyes for looking to see if anyone is watching. Tiny ears, unable to hear people telling them off or telling them to have more sense – and – most importantly – a very small head.

Sarah As this is the part that houses the very small brain?

Sue Strangely enough, no. This small head is too small to house a brain – just sensory equipment like eyes, nose, direction mechanism, etc. No, the brain needs a much bigger area in which to live – which, in the male, has to be the bottom.

Sarah Of course. The huge bottom of the male. Made huge due to lots of sitting on it whilst allowing the girls to do all the work. No effort being made to do any work themselves, you see.

Sasha The brain being in the bottom acts as an enormous weight, pulling the male into furniture, onto floors, etc., making it difficult to get up again for at least a few hours at a time.

Sue Or until the girls have done all the work.

Sasha That's just about it.

Sue As boys become men, they try to lever themselves out of chairs, settees, etc. by growing beer-bellies in an attempt to pull the body forward. However, this is not sensible and merely helps to weight them further into the chair.

Sasha This is always a problem with boys – having no sense, having too much weight pushing onto their brains and generally causing them to blunder about being foolish. Sue? The classroom situation?

Sue Thanks, Sasha. The classroom situation is really a good example. Walk into any classroom and the girls are aware – talking to each other, reading, writing – generally being aware enough to know that things have to be done. However, the boys are not aware even of where they are and, therefore, are staggering about, doing impressions of animals and trying to grab at each other for a pretend fight.

Sarah If we take a look at this video, (*switches on video*) here we have an empty classroom. On a table, we placed a book. We asked a girl to walk in and sit at the table. As you can see, the girl walks in. – There, she sits at the table – and – yes, as you can see she is immediately aware that there is a book there and that it might be worth reading. And – yes, she flicks through the pages. – Now, the girl leaves, the room is set up again, with the book closed on the table ready for the boy to come in. – And here he comes – bursting through the door and hurling himself against the wall, pretending to be some kind of soldier, spy, ape-man – whatever. He sees the book – picks it up and – yes, he puts it on his head, thinking it is a rain-hat. Pitiful, really.

Sasha Because when given work within the community, males cannot cope – just in the same way that they think a book is a rain-hat.

Sue Fortunately, the deeply intelligent and aware females are always there to take over and put things right.

Sarah Take females out of the community and society would collapse, the males spending all their time fighting each other and putting books on their heads.

Sasha Who makes war?

Sarah The male.

Sue Who believes that fighting solves everything?

Sasha The male.

Sarah When was the last time you saw a male with a book?

Sue When it was raining.

Sasha The difference between boys and girls, therefore, is biological.

Sarah	Girls are superior and aware –
Sue	Because boys sit on their brains.
Sasha	Thank you. Any questions? No? Very well. After break, we will be raising the second issue for presentation this morning, which is 'Stereotyping: Are We Aware Of What We Are Saying?'

GROUNDED

Cast: *Greg, Mum's partner*
Mum
Dav, Mum's teenage daughter
Ash, Mum's teenage son

Scene: *The living-room. Midnight. Mum and Greg*
are waiting up for Ash who is late home.

Greg   He's dead.

Mum   Oh, Greg, don't.

Greg   Don't what?

Mum   Don't get yourself all upset.

Greg   I'm not upset. I'm furious!

Mum   It's only midnight.

Greg   Only midnight?! Do you know how many killers and
nutters there are out on the streets these days in
broad daylight – never mind midnight!

Mum   But he's fifteen. We've got to give him some space.

Greg   When Ash went out of the house tonight, WHAT
time did he say he'd be back?

Mum   Eleven.

Greg   And WHAT time is it now?

Mum   All right.

Greg   And WHAT time is it now, I said?

Mum   All right, all right – midnight! There? Happy now,
are you?

Greg   Right. Midnight. So he lied to me. Right. So he gets it.

Mum   You're just a bully these days, Greg.

Greg   Well, if I don't discipline him, you won't. Will you?

Mum   He's my baby.

Greg   Well, he's not mine. You're too soft with him. That's
why he's like this.

Mum	Don't blame me!
Greg	He's walking all over you!
Mum	He's just feeling his feet.
Greg	You want to sort your son out, never mind leaving it to me.
Mum	When you moved in, you said he was your son, too.
Greg	Well, I might have changed my mind.
	Silence.
Mum	I don't know what's happening to us.
	Enter Dav, in her nightwear T-shirt.
Mum	What are you doing up?
Dav	I can't sleep with the row you're making down here, can I?
Mum	Get to bed.
Greg	Leave her alone, Peg. Dav hasn't done anything.
Mum	Oh, right. Side with her.
Dav	Where's Ash?
Mum	Oh, stop pretending you don't know, Dav.
Dav	I DON'T know. Where is he?
Mum	Don't tell me you weren't listening like you always do.
Dav	I don't listen to your private conversations. I'm not interested.
Mum	Don't you come it with me, Madam!
Greg	Shut up, the both of you. Ash hasn't come back yet and he said he'd be back by eleven.
Dav	He'll be drunk by now, I'll bet.
Mum	Drunk? What an evil thing to say!
Dav	He's been drinking for ages. So Tessa says.
Mum	You want to tell Tessa to mind her own business before I tell her mother about that job she's got.
Dav	I'm just saying what she said.
Greg	He'd better not be drinking.
Dav	Are you going to ground him, Greg?

98

Mum	You mind your own business.
Dav	Tch! Sorry I spoke!
Mum	Grounded! I'm the one that's grounded. I'm stuck here with you lot.

Enter Ash.

Ash	What's this? The welcoming committee?
Greg	Well, look who's decided to wander back in, then!
Mum	Ash! See? I said he'd be fine.
Greg	Where have you been?
Ash	Out.
Mum	Out. There. You see? Did you have a nice time, love?
Greg	Out where?
Ash	Stuart's party. Like I said before I went out.
Greg	You said you'd be back by eleven!
Mum	We were worried, Son.
Ash	It's only midnight. I'm only an hour late. Oh, I'm not listening to this. I'm off to bed.
Greg	You stay where you are!
Dav	Yeah. You're gonna get it now.
Ash	Why don't you push off back to your coffin, Deadly?
Dav	Did you hear that, Greg?
Greg	You leave your sister alone!
Ash	Which would be more than the lads in her year do.
Dav	Greg!
Mum	What lads? Have you been messing about with lads, Dav? Have you?
Dav	No!
Mum	HAVE YOU?
Dav	NO, I said!! Tch! Deaf!
Mum	You'd better not have been! I don't want any disease or unwanted pregnancies in MY house!
Dav	YOUR house?! It's Greg's as well! He's got some say in this house, too, you know!

Mum	Oh, no, he hasn't! This is MY house! I pay the rent! He just moved in here!
Greg	Hey! That's enough from you an' all, Peg!
Mum	Enough? Enough?! I don't think it is enough! I've certainly heard enough from you lot, I can tell you that!
Greg	Oh, shut up, Peg!
Mum	Don't you tell me to shut up, Son!
Dav	Mum!
Mum	I'm sick of hearing everyone in this house going on and on! I'm sick of my daughter sucking up to my stinking boyfriend all the time and him telling me to shut up like he owns the place! Which he DOESN'T!
Dav	Don't you talk to Greg like that! He's the best thing that's happened to this family in a long time!
Mum	Oh, shut your stupid mouth! You don't know what you're talking about, girl!
Dav	Oh, yes, I do! Greg might be just living here, but he's been more of a dad than my father ever was!
Mum	Don't you talk about your father like that! You didn't know him!
Dav	I know I didn't know him! That's the point!
Mum	Shut it, I'm warning you!
Dav	You shut it!
Greg	This is all your fault, Ash!
Ash	Oh! I thought it would be. It's always my fault. Everything's my fault, isn't it?!
Greg	I hope you're proud of yourself upsetting everyone like this!
Ash	You've got no right to criticise me! You're not my father!
Greg	No. And I wouldn't want to be either.
Mum	You leave my son alone!
Greg	Leave him alone? I can do better than that. I can leave altogether!

He storms upstairs to pack.

Mum   Greg! Greg!

Dav   Now look what you've done!

Mum   Greg!

Dav   He's packing!

Ash   Shouldn't take him too long. How long does it take to shove a mirror and a scruffy pair of jeans in a carrier-bag?

Greg   (*coming back in*) I'm out of here. Family-life? You can stick it!

Greg walks out, slamming the door behind him.

Ash   Just when I thought nothing good could happen today.

Mum   What kind of a life is this?

Ash   One that just got better.

Mum   Don't you get smart with me!

Ash   Look, Mum. What is so bad about that creep walking out? We're better off without him.

Mum   YOU'RE better off without him. I'm just without him.

Ash   Then find somebody else.

Dav   Find somebody else?

Mum   What are you talking about, 'Find somebody else'? What do you think relationships are? A shopping-spree?

Ash   I don't know, but Mum, next time you go shopping – don't go to a jumble-sale. Goodnight.

Mum   Don't you cheek me! You've just ruined my life! Don't you walk away from me when I'm speaking to you! Where are you going?

Ash   Bed. I've got a lecture at nine.

Mum   Oh. Right. See you in the morning. And don't you worry about me and my blood-pressure!

Ash   You don't have blood-pressure.

Mum   Yes, I do! You're not a doctor. You wouldn't know anyway. You never ask me how I am. You don't care!

Ash If you've got blood-pressure, lose some weight and lay off the men for a while.

He leaves the room.

Mum How dare you speak to me like that! How dare you! You're a pig! You're just like your father! Did you know that? Well, don't you try going out again tomorrow night because you're grounded!!

Dav Is that it? Is that all you're gonna say to him? After all that's happened?

Mum What are you still up for?

Dav I can't stand living here. As soon as I'm old enough, I'm off. And I'm never coming back.

She goes upstairs.

Mum Shame!

Dav (*calling down*) I hate you!

Mum And you're grounded as well!

Bedroom door slams.

Mum (*sadly*) Like me.

COMMON

Cast: *Gad*
Fliss

Scene: *A room with a tape-recorder on a table. Two people face each other across the table. Gad presses 'Play' to begin the tape.*

Gad Text for this project?

Fliss Literature project.

Gad Literature project – is . . .?

Fliss *Pygmalion* – by . . .?

Gad George Bernard Shaw.

Fliss And it is about?

Gad The importance of money.

Fliss The importance of education.

Gad And the evils of the class system.

Fliss And what was Shaw's point in writing the play?

Gad That without money and education, a person could only have the lowest place in the class system.

Fliss Which meant that that person would be classed as . . .?

Gad Common.

Fliss So. Where do we start?

Gad With the story. I'll just look it up in my notes.

Fliss It's all right. I know it in my head.

Gad I'll look it up. Just to be sure.
Silence.

Fliss You mean, you don't trust me.

Gad (*reading from notes*) 'Eliza Dolittle, poor flower-girl from the lowest end of the class system, goes to Henry Higgins, an upper-middle-class language

	professor, for lessons on how to 'talk proper' so that she can become a lady in a flower shop.'
Fliss	I said, you don't trust me.
Gad	(*reading*) 'Higgins teaches her for six months and passes Eliza off as a duchess at the Embassy Ball. This also fulfils a bet he had with his friend Colonel Pickering, who bet him that he couldn't do it.'
Fliss	I could have told you that from memory. But you don't trust me because . . .
Gad	And then – to cut a long story short – he doesn't know what to do with Eliza after the experiment is finished. She's too educated now to go back to the gutter and too common to be a proper lady. And she turns on him. Like a dog.
Fliss	You sanctimonious snob.
Gad	What? I was just checking my notes, Stupid! You're touchy!!
Fliss	Common. You said it. Common.
Gad	When did I say you were common? When?
Fliss	You don't have to. I can see it in your eyes. I can hear it in the words you use: stupid, touchy, common.
Gad	When did 'touchy' become a common word?
Fliss	It's just another negative word that people like you use to keep people like me in their place.
Gad	Place! And what do you mean, 'people like you'?
Fliss	You think you're better than me! You know you do!
Gad	I do not think I'm better than you. Fliss – you're paranoid.
Fliss	I am not paranoid! Whenever I stand up for myself, you say I'm paranoid! It's just another way of making me look hysterical and stupid – and common.
Gad	Look, if you're going to be like this, I've got other people to work with, you know. People who'd rather like to work with me, actually.
Fliss	See? There you go again! Other people! – Yeah. I know which other people, too. Richard and Jessica.

Silence.

Gad That's not true.

Fliss It is true. The teacher made you work with me.

Gad Look, shall we get on with this?

Fliss If given the choice, you would have worked with the far superior Richard and the far more educated Jessica because you've got FAR more in common.

Gad Really?

Fliss Really.

Gad And what might that be?

Fliss The fact that you use language carefully like 'What MIGHT that be?' and 'SHALL we get on with this?' to show that you are POSH.

Gad Nonsense.

Fliss There! There you go again! 'Nonsense' instead of 'Rubbish' or 'Garbage'. You're very carefully telling me that you're DIFFERENT to me. That you're BETTER than me.

Gad Based on what? Go on. Say it.

Fliss You say it. It's your problem.

Gad No. You say it. You started this. You and your 'rubbish' paranoia and your 'Garbage' philosophy on life. Because I've got more money than you. That's it, isn't it? Well, I'm AWFULLY sorry, OLD BEAN, that my father is a doctor and yours works in a factory! Excuse ME for having the AUDACITY to be born into a well-off family!! Perhaps I should have swapped UTERUSES with you! Or do you prefer WOMBS?

Silence.

Gad You know your problem, don't you? You're jealous.

Silence.

Gad Aren't you?

Fliss You disgust me. I'm only working with you because I have to.

Gad Why? Why do I disgust you? Because I speak what I feel? Because I dare to support what I am? Well-off?

105

Why should I be ashamed of being well-off? My father works very hard for his money.

Fliss So does mine!

Gad I'm sure he does.

Fliss And my mother works!

Gad I'm sure she does. But that's not my point. You want me to feel ashamed of being middle-class. Well, I don't. I don't think in those terms. I'm a person whose father is a doctor. I live the life I live because we have the amount of money my father makes to spend. You act like I got the money by magic and that YOU should have it by rights of equality or something. Like, why should I have all the money when you haven't got any?

Fliss Your father is a doctor because he had the advantage of a good education which my father and mother never had. And my father and mother never had a good education because they were stuffed into the local comp when your father automatically went to grammar school because of how much money he had.

Gad My father got into grammar school purely because he passed the entrance exam.

Fliss My father was refused a place at the grammar school even THOUGH he passed the entrance exam. There was only one place left and so they gave it to the lad whose father was the local bank manager.

Gad Prove it.

Fliss You mean, you don't trust me.

Gad I mean prove it.

Fliss You are so arrogant. Typical of your class. Safe with your money and education and looking down on the rest of us.

Gad And you are angry. Typical of your class. Threatened by anybody who has anything more than you've got.

Fliss Than you HAVE.

Gad   Correcting my English makes you feel better, does it, Fliss?

Fliss   You MIGHT say that, yes, Gad. It just reveals a chink in the old armour.

Gad   The armour being . . .?

Fliss   Fear.

Gad   Of what?

Fliss   Of what your class has created. The under-dog. Just like Pygmalion created Galatea. Just like Higgins created Eliza. And you know the old saying, don't you? 'Every dog will have his day.'

Gad   MUST have his day.

Silence.

Fliss   You're so common.

She switches off the tape-recorder.

Sketches

WORKSHOP SKETCHES

The purpose of these scripts is for the pupils to discuss and express considered opinions in pairings/groups in order to establish characters, settings, moves – if performed – and generally express clear points of view with regard to interpretation. The interpretation of these scripts depends entirely upon their own imagination and reasoning.

The format for working with each script is quite basic. A written response may be given to formalise pupil's thinking and what they have gained from the activity, but the teacher may use these scripts in any other way they consider suitable for the needs of their pupils.

BASIC FORMAT FOR USE

SPEAKING AND LISTENING/READING

1 Read through the script with as many in the group as required.
2 Decide on who or what you are playing by interpreting the words you are reading. Is it a person, an animal or an inanimate object? What is your reasoning for this? Explain to the others you are working with. Who you are defines who they are, so you all have to agree.
3 Where are these characters as they speak? Again, what is your reasoning for this? When read/performed the play has to make sense. If you believe that all this talk of sea and a desire for fish makes you and your friend seals, then you cannot be on a street. Look for clues in the script.
4 Re-read the script now with appropriate voices for your characters and, if performed, moves.
5 Different pairings/groups may have different interpretations, which is something that the whole group may discuss afterwards, in addition to what has been learned from or enjoyed about doing this activity.

WRITING

1 Write a clear account of the activity you have just taken part in. Use the process itself as your structure, explaining simply and clearly each stage of the activity.

2 Give your opinions and feelings about the activity. Did you enjoy doing it? What did you gain from taking part in it? Was it a different experience to reading the other, longer scripts in which you are told who you are playing, what the setting is, etc? Explain.

3 Which type of script do you prefer reading? Give reasons.

THINKING

Cast: *2*

A   What are you doing?

B   Thinking.

A   What for?

B   I like it. All your great philosophers think.

A   Like who?

B   Oh . . . Aristotle.

A   And?

B   Er . . . Plato. You know. The Greats.

A   Plato? Wasn't that Mickey Mouse's dog?

B   That's Pluto! Genius!

A   All right, all right. Keep your hair on. (*pause*) I'm a doer myself. You're a thinker, I'm a doer.

B   A doer? You? You're a couch-potato who doesn't even know the name of Mickey Mouse's dog!

A   I do! It's Plato!

B   Pluto! Oh, just shut up and go away.

A   I am a doer, then.

B   Like what? Name me one thing that you do apart from sleep, stuff your face and watch the telly.

A   I . . .

B   Go on.

A   I collect spiders.

B   You never!

A   I do, then! I've got a tarantula, I have.

B   Let's have a look.

A   What? And disturb your thinking, Aristotle? (*exits*)

B   I've finished thinking for today. It's given me a headache. Oy! Spiderman! Wait for me!

    B runs after A.

PLACE

Cast: *3*

A   I need a cigarette.

B   You can't have one.

A   I'm desperate.

B   It says over there. On the wall. 'No Smoking'. So you can't.

A   It also says over there 'No Dogs'. So you'd better get out now. Before They catch you.

B   They don't bother me.

A   They bother everybody. That's why we're here.

B   (*seeing C enter*) Hello. Another visitor. (*to C*) What you been up to, then?

C   Mind your own.

B   Oh. Hard man. Must be a murderer.

C   Don't be daft. I'd be lasered by now if I were a murderer, wouldn't I?

A   Jez got lasered yesterday.

B   Never! Jez? Who'd he kill?

C   No one. Jez never killed no one.

A   How do you know?

C   I lived with him.

B   Oh, yeah? Makes sense.

C   Meaning?

B   Meaning the flat-mate's usually the one to grass the other one up to the SNEDS. Good money to be made there. For the very expensive rent.

C   Take that back before I knock your head clean off!

A   Keep your voices down, the both of you. Do you want to be spike-trapped? Do ya?

B   I'll speak me mind!

Pause.

C They caught him stealing water.

A Who? Who was stealing water?

C Jez. I told him not to – but he never listened to anybody, did he?

A How much did you have left?

C Enough for the week. Then we'd have to join The Aquarius Queue.

A How come you're here?

C They traced me from his ID. Easy enough. Got stamped as an accomplice. Look. On my arm. The bleeding's stopped at least.

Pause.

A I need a cigarette.

Pause.

B What kind of place is this these days?

A It's Theirs.

STUCK

Cast: *2*

A   I'm cold.

B   You're always cold.

A   When they leave the door open, the draught cuts right through me.

B   So you've said. About twenty times in the last half-hour.

   Pause.

A   I wish I could close the door. It'd keep the heat in the room.

   Pause.

A   Then I wouldn't be cold.

   Pause.

A   I'm bored.

B   Will you shut up?! If it's not one thing, it's another. Yesterday you were too hot and restless!

A   Ah, well, they had the radiators turned up too much.

B   Well, do something about it, then!

A   How can I?

B   Well – just – just look out of the window or something. Watch the traffic going by. Count how many people with funny hair-cuts go past the gate. It'll take your mind off it.

A   Off what?

B   Off being cold and bored!

A   Oh, well, you've just gone and reminded me about it now, haven't you?

   Pause.

B   Just my luck to be stuck with you.

A   Thanks.

B You're nothing but a moan. Morning, noon and night.

A Well, pardon me for breathing. I shall keep my thoughts to myself in future.

B Good.

Pause.

A I wish someone'd put the telly on.

B Why?

A There's usually something good on this time of day.

B In the morning?! Daytime television?! You're joking! Like what?

A Cookery programmes.

B Please!

A I reckon I could make one of those dinners like they do, no trouble at all.

B In your dreams!

A I suppose so. It's not fair. One day though.

B I don't think so. Oh, look. Somebody's shut the door at last.

Pause.

A I'm hot.

B Oh, shut up!

PROGRAMME

Cast: *4*

A I think that it is –

B Only right –

C That we should –

D Stick together on this.

A You see! We've done it again!

B What?

A We're all talking –

C The same sentence.

B Are we?

C Well, not all the time.

D See. We didn't that time. Phew! Thank goodness! I've had a whole sentence to my –

A Self.

D Oh, damn it!

B Look, what's gone –

C Wrong?

D Is it our circuits –

C Or something?

A It might be the –

B Programme –

C Or maybe the entire system has completely –

D Gone haywire.

A This has got to be sorted –

B Out.

C We've all got things to –

D Do.
   Pause.

B Zzzzzzzzz – t!

A What's happened?

C I think there's been some shorting of –

D Circuits.

B Zzzzzzzzz – t!

A (*to B*) A73/421 !

C (*to A*) No response. Try –

D Zzzzzzzzz – t!

A (*to C*) Send out Emergency Code 347!

C No response! No – Zzzzzzzzz – t!

A Access to Database 3! Request access! – System in . . . distress . . . need . . .

ITCH

Cast: *2*

A Ow!

B What?

A Urgh!

B Well? You have my attention now. What do you want?

A I've got an itchy back.

B Oh, go away.

A I have. Really.

B So? What do you want me to do? Call for an ambulance?

A You wouldn't scratch it for me, would you?

B You're right. I wouldn't.

A Oh, please. I'd do it for you.

B Urgh! The very idea! Get lost!

A That's very cruel, that is.

B Oh? Cruel, am I? And whose fault is it that we're here in the first place? Eh?

A Sorry.

B What?

A SORRY! I've said it about a million times already!

B Well, say it again anyway!

A Sorry. Everso. I am. So – will you scratch my back?

B No!

A Tut!

Pause.

A I think I'm allergic to something in here.

B Well, there's a big choice of TWO things you can be allergic to in here. Dirt and rats.

A I've never been allergic to dirt . . . RATS?! Where? Where?

B There. In the corner. There's a big hole in the wall.

A I can't see any rats. OO! THERE'S ONE!

B Not any more. You've just frightened it back into the hole.

A Oh, dear.

B And stop snuggling up to me.

A I'm TIED to you! It's not snuggling up. I can't help it.

B Go away.

A I wish I could. I'd leave you here with the rat. You're pulling the same face.

Pause.

B Playing cards.

A Oh, not again! I was NOT!

B You were! And THAT'S why we're here!

A I didn't know it was against the rules. And I wasn't playing with them, I was counting them.

B Rubbish. It'll be ages before they let us out.

A Still – there's one good thing, anyway.

B What's that?

A That rat's frightened my itch away.

B Oh, well, that's all right, then!

CHIT-CHAT

Cast: *2*

A Ah! There you are, old boy!

B Lovely to see you again!

A Been ages.

B Haven't seen you since . . .

A Must have been . . .

B Treadmore's do.

A Treadmore's! Of course.

B Drink?

A No, thanks.

B Eats?

A No. Watching the old waistline, you know.

B So, how's business?

A Not bad. Mustn't grumble. Sold ten last week.

B Bravo.

A Got another fifteen being polished up to ship off next week.

B Good for you. Not doing so badly myself.

A So I heard. Lucky devil. Mind you, your stock is superior to mine.

B I have a good contact.

A You must let me have his name.

B His? HER.

A Really? Shipping out their own stuff now, are they?

B Very canny they are, too.

A Really?

B Yes. Got to have your wits about you working with them.

A Had some problems?

B She tried to push an absolute shrew onto me a month ago.

A Bad news.

B Indeed. I said, 'Look here. Don't try and push your reject goods onto me, Girly,' I said.

A Quite right.

B She read my anger anyway and pulled out a blonde.

A Much more saleable.

B Indeed.

A You've just got to watch them.

B They've got to know their place.

CLASS

Cast: *3*

A   What's the lesson today?

B   Class.

C   Meaning?

A   Could mean 'class' meaning stylish and sophisticated.

B   Or 'class' meaning class-system, meaning where you belong in society depending on how much money you've got or were born with.

C   Or 'class' meaning a class of kids.

A   Or it could be a misprint on the sheet and really read 'Glass'.

B   Meaning?

A   Meaning see-through substance used for windows and drinking out of.

C   And for spectacles to see out of windows and see what you're drinking.

B   True.

A   I hope it's about the class-system. I know lots about that. I'm upper-class, you know.

B   Upper-class without the money, title or birthright.

A   Or collection of big cars.

C   Or several select yet big houses.

B   Or the Swiss bank account.

A   True.

B   So, basically, you're poor.

A   But in an upper-class kind of way. I'm poor, but with a lot of swagger.

B   I'm poor with a lot of holes in my socks.

C   But you still have a lot of class.

B   Do I?

C   Oh, yes. You're very sophisticated.

B Do you think so?

C When you swig from a bottle, you always hold your little finger up.

B True.

A And when you have a good cough, you always do it into your jumper.

C Manners.

A And consideration for others.

B True.

C Shall we go to this 'Class' lecture, then?

A No. It's such a lovely day.

B I think we should take a stroll to the Art Gallery.

C Have a protest to the woman at the desk that we have a perfect right to be there.

A Being members of the public.

B And it IS free admission.

C Then get thrown out.

A Then see if Marco has any pizza he doesn't want.

B Good old Marco.

C He's such a gent.

A Let's go, then.

B Mind that broken glass.

C Well, whoever left that there?

A In the middle of the pavement!

B Some people have no class.

C True.

OWNERSHIP

Cast: *2*

A   Give me that!

B   No!

A   It's mine!

B   No!

A   Give it me NOW!

B   I want it! It's mine!

A   You didn't pay for it!

B   It's still mine. You've got no proof it's yours.
Silence.

B   Have you?

A   If you don't give that thing to me, I'll squash you so flat, the Reject Pizza Company won't even want you!

B   It's lovely. I shall love OWNING this. Being the rightful OWNER.

A   You're asking for a slap. You really are.

B   Being entitled to own it as I FOUND it. Poor little thing. All on its own.

A   It wasn't on its own. I'd only gone off to get it a drink.

B   It can't drink.

A   A CYBER-DRINK, stupid!

B   I had to fix it when I found it. It was weep-leaking.

A   It was weep-leaking because you picked it up!

B   And I thought to myself, poor little thing. Nobody wants you. Nobody OWNS you. I'LL look after you. So, now I DO. I OWN it. So there!

A   I saved up for that!

B   PROVE it.

A   I can't.
Silence.

A You own everything.

B I keep finding things lying around.

A You can't own everything you find!

B Finders-keepers. Losers-weepers.
Silence.

A I'm going to destroy it.

B What?

A I'm going to crush it into a quarter of kayli cyber-dust with my foot.

B Kill it?! No! I'm hanging onto it.

A I'll crush it IN your hand or OUT of your hand. It's up to you.

B No! You stay away from it!

A Put it down or you'll get hurt.

B Leave it alone! It hasn't done anything to you!

A Move. I'm warning you.

B Don't kill it! Look – have it back.

A I don't want it back. It's soiled goods now YOU'VE touched it.

B You've no right to do this! It's –
Silence.

A Losers-weepers.

FATE

Cast: *3*

A   When do you think it will drop on us?

B   What?

A   What do you mean, 'What?' ?! (*points upwards*)
     That! That thing up there!

B   Dunno. Don't care.

A   Don't care?! How can you not care?

B   I think if it's meant to drop on us, it will. If not, it'll
     go away.

C   Fate.

A   Oh. You've woken up at last, have you?

C   I wasn't asleep. I was thinking.

A   Not about very much, I'll bet.

C   Not really, no. I was thinking about you.

B   What do you mean, 'fate'?

C   Fate is what you just said. You said if it's meant to
     happen it will. That's fate.

A   I don't accept fate. I will not accept being dropped
     on by that thing!

B   Crushed. You mean crushed.

C   Obliterated.

B   Oh, yeah. A much better word.

A   Oh! Well, excuse ME, Dictionary Corner, for not
     getting the word right! The point is, it's going to do it
     whatever you call it!

B   Right. It's fate. So, why fight it?

A   Because it hasn't happened yet and we could get
     away from it.

C   Get away from it? Have you seen the size of it?

A   We could TRY!

B Try and get away from something you can't get away from?

A Yes!

B Why?

A Because we just might succeed!

B No, we won't.

C Look – who put it there?

A She did.

C Right. And why did she put it there?

A To get rid of us.

C And how badly does she want to get rid of us?

A Very badly.

C Exactly. So it's going to drop on us. The End. So shut up.

A But –

C No buts about it. Look, there's another one over there. She's put them everywhere if you hadn't noticed.

B It's fate all right. It's only a matter of time.

Silence.

A I'm gonna make a break for the 'fridge!

B That's crazy-talk!

C Don't do it!

A I can't take any more of this waiting! I'll take a chance!

B But –

A No buts about it! I've gotta do it! I was born to be crazy! I was meant to do this! It's FATE!

A runs off.

B So – when do you think it'll drop on US?

THERE

Cast: *2*

A Look, stand there, will you, love?

B What? Here?

A No, no. – God! Amateurs! – No, love. By the tree.

B Oh. Here?

A Yes. That's right.

B Soz. Didn't understand you.

A That's all right. Now – pick up the apple and face the front.

B Like this?

A No. He Two will see you coming a mile off like that, won't he? Look – it'd be easier to do this without eating.

B It's a lovely apple.

A Yes. I know. But we want to save some, don't we?

B Do we?

A For HIM, love. For HIM.

B Oh. Couldn't you spare another one?

A No, I could not! They don't grow on trees, you know.

B Yes, they do.

A Just face that way with the apple, will you?! Grief!

B Okay. Right. I'm doing that. Now what?

A Look alluring. Attractive.

B Even more so than I already am?

A Yes. God!

B Oo! Stop swearing! That's naughty, that is. He One won't like it.

A So what?

B And I don't think He One'll like me talking to you.

A Why not?

B   Well, I'm not supposed to come anywhere near this tree. I can go anywhere else, but not near this tree.

A   Why not? It's a nice tree.

B   I know.

A   Nice apples.

B   I know.

A   And think of how much more clever you're about to become. Just by eating that apple.

B   I've always wanted to be brainy. He Two gets cross with me sometimes. But, frankly, I think oranges taste nicer with the peel left on. And ant-stew is lovely – once you get used to it. Once you've found enough ants. He Two says I'm a waste of a rib.

A   He'll like you loads when he's had a bit of that apple.

B   You reckon?

A   So don't eat all of it.

B   Okay.

A   Look! Here he comes now!

B   Oo! Isn't this exciting? Just like when I dropped that huge rock accidentally on He Two's foot and he hopped about really thrillingly.

A   Right. I'm going to hide back up here in the leaves. You be all alluring now so that he comes over for a bit of the apple. Okay?

B   Okay. If you really think it'll work.

A   Oh. It'll work all right.

MOVE

Cast: *3*

A   Oy! Move!

B   Eh? What?

A   I know you're not asleep. Move.

B   I am asleep, then.

A   Not any more, you're not. Shift.

C   Leave her alone!

A   Who said that?

C   Me. Up here. Leave her alone, you bully.

A   Mind your own business! Who asked you?

C   Watch it. I can cause you an awful lot of grief from up here, you know.

A   I don't think so. Not in that cage you can't.

C   Don't underestimate me, mate.

A   (*to B*) Haven't you moved yet?! SHIFT!

B   It's not fair! I was here first!

C   Yeah! She was there first.

A   (*to C*) Stay out of this, you.

B   There's an unwritten law: first one to the fire gets the best spot.

A   Unwritten law? Unwritten law?! Who told you that? Got a solicitor, have we?

B   I was here first and I'm – and I'm not moving. So there!

C   Yeah! You tell him!

A   'So there'? Oh, I'm really frightened now!

B   You can still be by the fire. You'll be plenty warm enough by the coal scuttle.

C   Yeah. It's nice by the coal scuttle.

A   (*to C*) Listen you. I've told you to shut it. So shut it.

C No.

A No?

C No. You can't get me. You can't jump up this high.

A He cleans you out tomorrow. And I'll be waiting.

C I do not think so.

A (*to B*) Okay. You've got five seconds – and then I'm going to bite you.

B You wouldn't!

A Why not?

B Because – because I'd scratch you. Horribly. Deeply. Like with blood.

Silence.

A Stay there then. But you'd better check the shadows from now on. Because I'll be waiting in them.

C 'Bye.

A (*to C*) And YOUR days are numbered. Start counting!

A walks off.

C (*to B*) Congratulations. You won.

B I'm not so sure.

C I've never seen him move so fast.

CLEVER

Cast: *4*

A Who's clever, then?

B Me.

C I don't think so.

D Who asked you?

C Oh. Sticking up for him again.

D No. Just stating a fact.

A That's enough, you two. I demand that my question be answered.

B It has been. Me. I am clever. I am the cleverest person here.

C Based on what?!

B Based on the fact that I have the largest head with the largest brain in it.

C Is that right?

B Plus I am still all in one piece. Unlike the rest of you.

D That's true. Very true.

C See? There you go again! Sticking up for him!

D But it's true! Have YOU still got all your legs?

C Er – in what sense?

A Stop avoiding the question.

C Oh! OH! You're on their side, are you?

A Answer the question.

C I technically have the number of legs that I should have.

A Technically?

D Rubbish. I know I've got three less. And I've got a couple of ears missing.

A I've got at least two noses missing that I can't account for.

B　To lose one nose is unfortunate. To lose two is a blow.

D　(*to B*) You're so clever, I don't think.

C　(*to A*) You DID have a bad cold recently, you know.

A　That's true. I must take more Vitamin C.

D　Colds? Oh, don't remind me! With my last one, I sneezed so hard I blew myself inside out!

C　I remember that!

D　(*to A and C*) You two were very kind to me that day, sorting me out like you did.

A　Oh, that's all right.

C　No trouble at all.

B　Oy! What about me? What about going back to me being the cleverest?

A　(*to B*) Oh, be quiet!

D　(*to B*) Big-Head!

FASHION

Cast: *2*

A How do I look?

B Terrible.

A What?

B You look really stupid in that.

A I've just paid out a load of money for this outfit!

B You were robbed.

A This outfit is very fashionable, ACTUALLY. Everyone's wearing stuff like this.

B Where? Outer space?

A Get lost.

B I'd get my money back if I were you.
Silence.

A What's the matter with purple crushed-velvet waders?

B You look like a fisherman on a night out.

A Oh, shut up.

B And that pointed helmet looks like someone should be throwing hoops over it at the fairground for a penny a go.
Silence.

A Really?

B Really.

A Well, you'd better come back to the shop with me. I feel foolish enough as it is.

B Okay. I'll just put my new fluorescent pink ski-boots on. Do you like them?

A Agh! They're GHASTLY!!

B What? Nonsense. You've just got no sense of fashion.

LOVE

Cast: *2*

A Hey.

B What?

A I love him over there.

B Which one?

A Him. The one with the blue T-shirt.

B Him?! You can't love him!

A Why not?

B He's got a tattoo of a gorilla on his forehead!

A Not him! HIM! The one next to him!

B With the curly red hair?

A Yes.

B And the eye-patch?

A That's not an eye-patch! That's a shadow!

B Off what?

A Off the bloke standing next to him wearing the big hat.

B Oh.

A Do you like him?

B No. It's not a very nice hat, is it? A bit floppy.

A Not HIM! My chap with the red hair!

B Oh. No. I don't like him either.

A Why not?

B He's handcuffed to the bloke in the floppy hat.

A Is he? Oh. Shame. – Wait a sec. Just look at him in the jeans! I'm in love!

FANCY

Cast: *2*

A   Girls fancy me.

B   What? All of them?

A   All the ones I've met, yes. It's my great charm and good looks.

B   Name one.

A   One what?

B   Never mind stalling for time. Name one girl that fancies you.

A   Er – oo, there's such a lot to choose from.

B   One'll do.

A   Er – Emma.

B   What?! She does NOT!

A   She does. She's always sitting in front of me in class.

B   No. You're always following her and sitting behind HER.

A   Zena. Zena said I had a lovely face.

B   She said you had an UGLY face. You don't listen, you don't.

A   Michelle!

B   I do not think so.

A   Michelle said she'd like to look at the stars with me.

B   Michelle said if you didn't leave her alone she'd make you SEE stars.

A   Jodi! Jodi said she'd like to go on a rocket-trip with me.

B   She said she was going to boot you into orbit.

A   Well – they don't know what they're missing.

B   Yeah, right, He-Man. Just shut up and help me with this next sum.

A   Let's ask Emma! She can admit to fancying me at the same time! Er – Emma?

TOO

Cast: *3*

A   What do you think?

B   Too big.

C   For the room. And too wide.

A   Never get it through the door, will we?

B   What about this?

C   No! Too bright!

A   Against the blue.

B   I suppose so.

C   That's nice.

A   What? Too small!

B   Far too small.

C   Really?

A   You couldn't even get a cup on it.

B   No. It's got to be bigger.

C   But not too big.

A   Oh, this is really irritating. Let's have something to eat. We'll try again later.

B   Okay. Fish and chips?

C   Too greasy.

A   Pizza?

B   Too fattening.

C   Salad?

A   Too boring.

B   Look, will somebody make a decision around here!!

QUEUE

Cast: *4*

A   How long have we been here?

B   Since Friday.

C   Where's my flask? My flask has gone!

D   Be quiet. No one's got your flask.

A   (*to C*) I think it's under your blanket.

B   (*to C*) Behind your hot-water bottle.

C   Oh. Yes. Thanks.

D   This pavement's hard. And cold.

A   This is stupid. Why do I want that wet-look coat with the fake-fur leopard collar?

B   Why do I want that pair of armchairs with matching footstools?

C   Where's my chocolate? My chocolate has gone! I need it!

D   You need a kick in the pants.

A   (*to C*) Here. Have some of mine.

B   (*to C*) I know we've been here ages, but just keep calm.

C   CALM?! I'm CALM! No one's calmer than me!

D   (*to C*) It's all right, mate. Not long to go now.

A   I can't feel my feet any more.

B   Look! There's someone at the door!

C   There is! There is! The door's actually opening! We're saved!!

D   Someone help me up. I've got cramp.

A   (*to D*) I'll help. Wait a second! Look at those two!

B   They've jumped the queue! Let's get them!

C   Battle stations!! Where's my FLASK?!

FILE

Cast: *2*

A Ready?

B Yes.

A Right. – The white sheet is stapled to the blue and filed with the green.

B Why?

A Because those three go together for the Chief Administrator.

B The colours mean something, do they?

A Pay attention. They get filed in one of these plastic files with the logo in the corner.

B And then get put into the Chief Administrator's filing-cabinet?

A No. They then get put into this file-box with all the others.

B And then I take the file-box to the Chief Administrator?

A No. Then you have to go to the Filing Clerk who puts an official stamp on the file-box.

B And THEN I take it to the Chief Administrator.

A No. Then it has to have an official seal put on it.

B From the Official Seal Clerk.

A That's right. Have you worked here before?

B No. When DOES the Chief Administrator get the file-box?

A She doesn't.

B She doesn't?

A No. It's nothing to do with her.

B But it's her box! That's silly!

A No, no – you're so young – that's FILING.

B Ah.

QUIET

Cast: *2*

A Isn't it quiet?

B Ssh!

Silence.

A I like the quiet.

B So do I. So shut up.

Silence.

A The thing I like best about the quiet –

B Oh, dear . . .

A Is that you can't hear anything.

B Really? How deep. You thought about that for a long time, didn't you?

A I mean you CAN hear things . . .

B Like your fog-horn voice.

A But they're all lovely, quiet things . . .

B I feel a list coming on.

A Like the rain, the gentle breeze, the sea . . .

B The sea?! What are you on about? We're miles from the sea!

A But when it's really quiet, I can hear the sea – being carried to me by the gentle breeze, probably.

B You can hear the air circulating in the space between your ears. THAT'S what you can hear.

A You're very insensitive.

B You're very noisy.

A Oh, be quiet.

B I'd love to.

PEACE

Cast: *2*

A   Get away from me! Leave me alone!

B   But I want us to be friends!

A   How can we be friends when I don't like you?

B   Things can change.

A   After everything you've said to me in the past?

B   I've changed. Forgive and forget.

A   No.

B   I'm not the same as I was. – Peace, man.
    Silence.

A   Excuse me?

B   Peace.

A   Oh, dear.

B   What?

A   You've become a hippy. I knew it. I knew it when I
    saw the beads and the 'Love' badge.

B   I'm not a hippy. I just think peace is a good idea.

A   It is.

B   Great!

A   But not with you.

B   What's wrong with me?

A   You think peace is a fashion that you pull on with
    your tie-dye jeans. Well, it's not. Peace is a state of
    mind, not a change of clothes.

B   No. I think peace is what happens when you realise
    you were wrong. – Peace?

A   Take off the stupid gear and ask me tomorrow.

Activities

ACTIVITIES

AUDITION

SPEAKING AND LISTENING

How do Actor 1 and Actor 2 speak differently in the script? Notice the variation in language and in dialect, that is, the different words used to speak depending on which geographical area the speaker is from. Do any of the characters speak in Standard English? Do any of them use a regional dialect? When reading the parts, did you find that the language was forcing you into using a regional accent? Which words or phrases were making you do this?

READING

In your group, discuss the relationship between Actor 1 and Actor 2. Who are they? What kind of people are they? Are they related? Is this their first scam? What were their others, do you think? How much of what they tell The Director is actually true?

WRITING

Imagine you are an actor waiting to audition. Write a poem or short piece of prose based on how you feel. Think about:
- How it feels to wait in the wings
- How it feels to perform
- What your dream is
- What getting this job means to you.

FISH

SPEAKING AND LISTENING

Improvise a scene between two pets. They do not have to be fish, but there should be enough for them to 'talk' about. You could choose, for example:

- A cat and a mouse – the cat trying to get to a bird in its cage.
- Two exotic pets – a tarantula and a lizard stuck in a tank together.

READING

Read through the script a couple of times. Discuss with your partner what will happen next. Goldie is the inexperienced 'rookie' tank-tenant. Joey knows the ropes. What other dangers – such as The Pineapple-Chunks Catastrophe – could Joey steer them clear of?

WRITING

Write a scene involving the family that the fish belong to – the sometimes naughty, sometimes well-meaning children and the share-and-share-alike parents on their strict rota of household duties. Start, perhaps, with the son coming home from school with a bad report. How could this develop as a scene and culminate in a bad time for the fish?

WHEN

SPEAKING AND LISTENING

Improvise a scene between either:

- Jimmy and his parents, or
- Jimmy and his sister.

Emphasise whatever points you have picked up about their relationships from the script.

READING

Look at the way the script is structured. Information about Jimmy is revealed bit by bit until, by the end, a much more detailed picture is given of him.

Read through the script again and list in order all the things that are revealed about Jimmy. How does he appear to be at the beginning of the script? What have we found out that he is really like by the end of the script?

WRITING

Write an entry you might find in Jimmy's diary, describing his idea of a perfect day. Base your ideas on what is revealed about Jimmy's likes, dislikes, hopes and dreams in the script.

CRUSH

SPEAKING AND LISTENING

Sit back-to-back with a partner. One of you is Margie and the other is Marcus. Take it in turns to speak about how you get on with each other, the Valentine's card, how Margie fell over and Marcus helped and how much you think of each other. Will Marcus feel the same way about Margie as she does about him? Use appropriate voices and actions for these characters as you talk.

You should tap the other person inconspicuously to show that it is their turn to speak – that is, to cue them. Listen carefully to what each other says so that you are actually picking up on some point that they have made. Remember you are not talking *to* each other. You are talking *about* each other.

READING

Margie is a very romantic person. She likes to see the world in its very best light. She sees Marcus Jordaine in the same way.

- Look again at the script and list five things about Marcus that Margie finds romantic, stating why these things would be romantic to her.
- Pick out phrases and particular words that Margie uses which reveal her romantic view of life.
- Look at the end of the script. We learn something here about Margie. What is it? Is this why she is so romantic? Explain.

WRITING

Write the script of the scene that Margie describes when the cards were exchanged in the classroom. Remember to include the characters of Ian Turton, Samantha Fellows and the teacher. Your script should bring out the humour of the clash between Ian and Samantha, then the touching exchange between Margie and Marcus.

FORGETTING

SPEAKING AND LISTENING

There is a whole language of excuses for forgetting things. Work on an improvisation with your group. The basis of it should be that, in a line-up, one of you announces the thing you forgot and then, down the line-up, the rest of you should give some classic excuses for having forgotten this thing.

e.g. 'I forget to hand in my homework because . . .

- the dog ate it.'
- my little brother slopped his dinner on it.'
- I had to go to my auntie's last night and I left it there.'

Try to improvise about five different forgotten things. The more bizarre the excuses, the more interesting they are.

READING

As the narrator of the piece, Jason is talking directly to the audience.

- Which phrases or lines from the script express the idea that Jason wants you to understand and sympathise with him?
- Do you understand and sympathise with him? Is he like you or someone you know? What do you recognise about him and his family in your own life or in someone else's that you know?

WRITING

Imagine that you are Jason. You arrive at school having remembered your English book and football kit – but you have forgotten three other things! Write a script made up of three brief scenes about the consequences of having forgotten each of these three things.

BULLIES

SPEAKING AND LISTENING

In groups, improvise an incident of bullying. Discuss with your group the benefits of acting it out. Has it helped to make clear what might trigger an incident? Could it have been avoided? What is it about the bully that needs all this aggression?

Now discuss with your group how to improvise a scene where the bullied person wins.

READING

Choose one of the bullies in the sketch. Describe what you think they look like – hair, eyes, height, weight, any distinguishing features like scars, jewellery, tattoos, plus what they are wearing. How old do you think they are? Describe his /her family. Are they aggressive, too, or the total opposite?

WRITING

Write a newspaper article about the incident on the bus mentioned in the script. The clinical, journalisic style you use should make the crime more chilling.

Consider the structure you should use. The information given should be in a logical order. Here is a suggested structure:

- *Headline:* something suitably sharp and eye-catching.
- *Paragraph 1:* a short paragraph stating the incident that has taken place, including the time, date and place of the incident.
- *Paragraph 2:* a more detailed account of the incident.
- *Paragraph 3:* a statement from the person who was bullied.
- *Paragraph 4:* a statement from a witness on the bus.
- *Paragraph 5:* a statement from a police officer called to the scene or the manager of the bus company.
- *Paragraph 6:* what the police or authorities are intending to do about this incident.

FAULT

SPEAKING AND LISTENING

Discuss with your group the different natures of Cal and Maz. Use the following points to help further your discussion:

- When they talk, Cal is the most aggressive and Maz is the most passive. Why is this? Does it reveal anything about their individual family backgrounds?
- What are their different attitudes to authority?
- How do their attitudes towards the boy's injury differ?
- Why does Maz need to confess to what happened whereas Cal wouldn't dream of doing such a thing?

READING

Trace Maz's growing sense of guilt and responsibility using five quotations from the script Write down the quotations in order with a brief note next to each to explain its relevance. For example:

Cal	It's not my fault.	This shows that at the beginning of the script, Maz is very much in the same frame of mind as Cal – refusing to take any responsibility for what has happened.
Maz	It's not mine.	

WRITING

Write the script of the Headteacher's interview with Cal, then Maz, revealing the different attitudes of each pupil.

153

PUMPKIN

SPEAKING AND LISTENING

What ambitions do you have? Make a list of them, then sit with your group and pool this information. Are your ambitions similar? Are they to do with growing up – jobs, etc.? Are some of them to do with meeting people, travel, etc. ? When you have made your lists, do the boys have different ambitions from the girls? Is there a limit to the ambitions the group has or are some of them exciting and adventurous?

READING

Take a closer look at the script.

- Why is it structured in the way that it is?
- At which point did you suddenly realise that this was no ordinary pumpkin but a rather famous one? What clues were given to you in the script?

WRITING

Write a monologue for one of the mice involved in the magical transformation that night. What was its life like prior to being chosen to be part of the 'coach-party'? How did its life change afterwards?

POCKET-MONEY

SPEAKING AND LISTENING

Get into groups. Each person writes down gift items on slips of paper – some fantastic, some junk. Shuffle them and turn them face-down. Three slips are turned over. The group then has to imagine that instead of pocket-money they were given these three items to keep themselves amused with over the weekend. The more stupid the items, the more amusing will be the activities.

READING

Take a closer look at the script and itemise exactly what each member of the family wants to spend their 'pocket-money' on – including the adults.

- Is the 'pocket-money' about to be positively or usefully spent? Which character, in your opinion, will get the most from their spending? Explain your point of view with reference to the text.
- Bearing in mind her attitude and what she talks about in the script, if Nan were to have 'pocket-money', what would she spend it on? Would the money be more sensibly spent? Again, explain your point of view with reference to the text.

WRITING

Write the script of the chance meeting of Cynth and Tez and their respective dates later. Neither of them likes the other's date, so what happens? Is it something terrible to make matters worse, or something nice to bring the four of them together?

ORDER

SPEAKING AND LISTENING

What experience do you and your group have of restaurants?
Compile a list as you talk of the best and worst restaurants you have
ever been to, plus the best and worst meals you have ever had –
everything from a cold burger to lumpy custard. Did you complain?
Is it important to complain? Why?

READING

The waitress always has to be polite and efficient throughout
the script because that is her job. The language she uses is
'automatic' at times in that she has to say the same things to
customers every day. It is also very polite even though the
customers can be difficult. Give examples of both of these, using
quotations from the script.

WRITING

Write a letter from any character in the script – apart from Barry! – to
a problem-page agony-aunt. If you choose a member of the family,
you might complain about how your family behaved in the
restaurant that evening and how you just don't understand them. If
you choose the waitress, you might write about the pressures of the
waitressing job, giving as an example the other evening when you
had to wait on this family with the fussy mother, the sulky father and
the arguing kids.

FANS

SPEAKING AND LISTENING

Who do you admire? Prepare ten key points that say why this person is so important to you. You should also prepare an information sheet on this person to allow a group to question you in a two-minute hot-seating session.

READING

The characters in the script mention names and titles of pop stars, music and games. Take a closer look at the script. Are these names and titles odd or far-fetched? Or are they pretty standard for the types of odd or inventive names given to stars, bands, songs and games? Think about names that are around at the moment. What image are they giving to the band, star, game, etc? Do you think the names were chosen to sell that particular 'product'?

Now research bands, stars, etc. from 20 or 30 years ago. Were the names conveying a different image? Was this to suit or reflect different times?

WRITING

Prepare and write an information sheet on a person you admire for your school 'Idol Of The Week' article. You should include details of the idol's background, likes, dislikes, heroes, current success, ambitions, etc. so that your readers can get an instant picture of the person.

AWAY

SPEAKING AND LISTENING

- After reading Scene One, get into groups and predict what will happen in Scene Two. Make a few notes, then read Scene Two. How close were you? How does your ending compare to the actual ending?
- Have you ever been on a residential school trip? Tell your group what you did there and whether any of the other pupils played up. Allow the group to question you: What did you get out of the trip? Would you go again?

READING

This play is structured in two scenes. Its dramatic information is given out in a particular order so that the story is revealed to the reader in a certain way.

- Why do you think the play is in two scenes rather than three? For example, there could have been a middle scene which dramatised the actual educational activities the characters were involved in and what happened rather than just reporting them in Scene Two. Why was this not included?
- List the three most important story-points given to the reader in Scene One and then in Scene Two.
- How are the details and story-points in Scene One linked with those in Scene Two? Explain.
- What conclusions can you come to about how a play is structured?

WRITING

- Write a statement as if you were one of the characters in the script, defending yourself, your behaviour and the utter chaos caused at the end of the play.
- Alternatively, write a criticism of the play, commenting on whether it is fair that the boys should be portrayed in such a negative light.

US

SPEAKING AND LISTENING

What makes people want to be teachers? Work with a partner on devising ten questions to ask a teacher to find out more about why they wanted to be a teacher and what being a teacher is actually like. Discuss with your partner what you need to know and then decide on the questions. Avoid 'closed questions' that can only be given a yes or no answer, e.g. 'Do you like being a teacher?'

READING

Choose one teacher from the script. Explain what you think they might be like in the classroom compared to what they are like with their friends at dinnertime. Use quotations to support your opinions.

WRITING

Describe the classroom of one of the teachers in the script. Their surroundings should reflect what you think they are like as people, based on what you have picked up about them from the script. Comment on:

- The first thing that strikes you about the room as you walk into it.
- How the room is organised – tables in rows, groups, arcs? Is it neat?
- What posters are on the walls? Any other items of interest in the room?
- Is it a nice room? Unfriendly? Dull? Exciting?

FRIENDS

SPEAKING AND LISTENING

What is your friendship group like? Is it made up of different types of people who provide certain needs for the rest of the group? For example, is there a forceful one who keeps the rest of the group motivated? Is there a caring one who looks after people in the group when they are upset or unwell?

Next, see if you can work out how you all came to meet and why you stay together, even – perhaps – when you have more negative people in the group like Leanne in the script.

Just what is friendship? Can you define it?

READING

From what you know of Tom's character – what he says, what he does and what people say about him – why do you think he has no friends? Is Leanne right, or is there more to it than that? Write down your opinions.

WRITING

Write the script of the scene after school when the group meet at the cinema; unexpectedly, Leanne turns up, too. Why would she meet them there when she has finished with them? Take these characters a step further, using what you have learnt about them from the original script.

CARING

SPEAKING AND LISTENING

Improvise a back-to-back telephone call from Jay to Tina at the end of the play. Discuss the content with your partner beforehand, mapping out key points to cover from your reading of the script. Then improvise the piece. Organise the cueing of each other's turn to speak by inconspicuously tapping each other.

READING

Why is it difficult for Jay to express his true feelings even when he has so many people willing to help him? Look closely at the script for clues to what is making him 'block' people.

WRITING

The script is structured to show Jay being questioned by the people who care about him, then given an ultimatum to change for the positive. It ends with Jay accepting the positive choice. How else could the script have ended? Write another ending for the script.

FRUSTRATION

SPEAKING AND LISTENING

Think of a time when you had to compete with a friend – whether it was in a simple board-game, a team-sport, track-event or whatever. Tell the group about your experience and whether it changed the friendship, as it nearly does in the script.

READING

We meet the characters in the script through what they say, but what do they actually look like in your imagination? Write character descriptions of Tank, Gracie, Gismo and Cat based on your reading of the script. Explain why you think they got their nicknames.

WRITING

Write a script for the confrontation which might take place between Cat and Gismo at the end of the play.

GENTS

SPEAKING AND LISTENING

Discuss the attitudes of these three elderly characters. Shakespeare wrote a famous speech in *As You Like It* beginning 'All the world's a stage'. He said that we revert back to child-like attitudes and behaviour in old age. Is this true of the characters in the script? Give examples from the play. Do you know similar people to these in your own life?

READING

What is the relationship like between Fred and Edie? What is it based on? How do you think they met? What keeps them together? Support your ideas from the script.

WRITING

Write a statement from Edie about how she met Fred. Why did she marry him? What has life been like with Fred over the years? Has he changed at all? What does she think of his friends? What does she think of him now compared to the man she married?

GENDER

SPEAKING AND LISTENING

Discuss whether we really have stereotypical ideas about the opposite sex or whether we agree that both sexes are equal.

Use these headings to formalise the discussion and thinking within your group. You can break the examples down further in your discussion.

The Ways In Which We Are Equal

- The subjects we can take at school.
- The jobs/courses we can apply for.
- The right we have to speak our opinions.

The Ways In Which We Are Different

- Anatomical differences.
- Certain clothes we wear.
- The ways in which we move, sit, stand, etc.

Look at your completed lists. How reasonable are they? How many are genuinely your own views? How many are views that have been learnt from others?

READING

In groups, take another look at the script and argue which points, if any, made about males and females are actually true, and to what extent.

WRITING

Write a couple of paragraphs about the unfair treatment of males and females in the media – novels, plays, poetry, television, radio, films, magazines, computer games, etc.

GROUNDED

SPEAKING AND LISTENING

Have you ever been grounded? What had you done? Discuss in your group the different reasons for being grounded in all your different households. Is it easier to be grounded in some households than in others? What does being grounded mean? Does its definition vary in each household, too? Would you prefer another punishment, e.g. pocket-money being stopped, to being grounded? Share the main points made by your group formally with the rest of the class.

READING

Which character in the script do you think is the most unpleasant? Support your opinion with reference to what they say and do in the script.

WRITING

Imagine that matters got out of hand the next day when Greg came back for something. Write a police report from one of the officers called to the scene. Include:

- How, when and by whom the police were notified.
- The address at which the incident took place and details of what the police saw when they first arrived.
- Statements taken from people at the scene of the incident.
- Any action taken by the police.

Keep the language used in the report very formal and official, for example:

At 16.30 hours on Friday 12th September, I was requested to attend an incident at 33, Stuart Street on the Beckridge Estate. The station had received a telephone call from a neighbour, Mr Brian Thornhill, complaining about a fight . . .

COMMON

SPEAKING AND LISTENING

George Bernard Shaw believed that language was important in bringing about equality. He believed that if we all spoke 'correctly', that is, without a regional dialect or heavy accent, it would help to remove the barriers of prejudice and ignorance that he believed divided people. Do you agree? Are we prejudiced with regard not only to standards of education but also to accents and dialect? Discuss.

READING

'It's just another negative word that people like you use to keep people like me in their place.'

Take a closer look at the script. Is language used as a weapon by Gad and Fliss in order to hurt or label each other as being a certain kind of person? For example, Fliss calls Gad a 'snob'; Gad calls Fliss 'Stupid'.

- What do these words mean? How are they meant to offend?
- How powerful is name-calling and why? Are these words labelling people?
- List other examples of this negative use of language from the text, plus examples of language/names most likely to offend or cause friction in your school, and try to explain why they offend so much.

WRITING

Write a formal piece on how language can sometimes be a unifying force, such as how slang can be a kind of 'youth-speak'.

Slang is an ever-changing form of language. It was originally a secretive language used by the criminal community to prevent the law-officials from understanding what they were talking about. However, slang has now become the fashionable language of the young. Across the globe, the same key words are used by young people who speak the same language, identifying themselves as having something in common – the fact that they are young.

Consider the following points in your writing:

1 What words do you and your friends use when you talk amongst yourselves?

- If someone is 'safe', it means that they are admired and accepted.
- If one friend 'skanked' another friend, it means that they are ignoring them and going off with someone else.

2 Where do we pick up new slang words: from television, radio, magazines, new friends?

3 Do you use slang when talking to adults?

4 Does it sound odd when adults try to use your slang?

5 Why is it important to have slang?